Prayers That God Hears

By
Dr. Henry G. Covert

Prayers That God Hears
by Dr. Henry G. Covert

Copyright © 2022
All rights reserved.

Library of Congress Number: 2022948806
International Standard Book Number: 978-1-60126-828-0

Masthof Press
219 Mill Road | Morgantown, PA 19543-9516
www.Masthof.com

Prayers That God Hears

Henry G. Covert

Acknowledgment

This book is dedicated to my wife Katherine, whose support and encouragement is a motivator for my writings.

Contents

Introduction 9

Chapter One: Foundations for Prayer 13
    The Vine and Branches 14
    Marriage Analogy 15
    Knowing God's Will 17
    The Lord's Prayer 19
    Intercession of the Holy Spirit 46

Chapter Two: Approaching God 51
    The Struggle 51
    Prayers of the Heart 54
    Solitude and Silence 56
    Praying in Faith 59
    Prayers for Healing and Miracles 63
    Reasoning with God 69
    Repentance and Humility 72
    Righteous Relationships 78
    Persistent and Fervent Prayer 85
    Praise and Thanksgiving 87
    Communal Prayer 91
    Praying in Jesus' Name 93

Chapter Three: Content of Prayer 97
    Gift of Love and the Spirit 97
    Praying for Enemies 100

Patience	104
Prayer for Healing	108
Sustaining Grace	110
Deliverance from Temptation	113
Increased Faith	115
Understanding and Wisdom	117
Praying for the Saints	119
Prayer for the Needy	121
Christian Unity	124
Conclusion	127
Appendix	131
Resources	139

Prayers That God Hears

Introduction

It is prayer that ignites the compassion and power of God, establishing and nurturing a relationship between us and the Almighty. The Bible tells us about individuals of humility and faith who received powerful responses to their prayers. For example, Hannah, who was distressed by the personal insults resulting from her being childless, prayed to the Lord for a son. God answered her plea, and she bore Samuel who became a great servant and leader of the people. It was the prayer of Moses that brought forth water in the wilderness to sustain the life of the Israelites. His prayers also saved the people from God's wrath when they fashioned a false deity. Joshua's prayer caused the sun to stand still over Gibeon and the moon over the valley of Aijalon, until Israel established victory over its enemies. These are but a few instances when God responded with power to the cries of his children. (Exodus 17:1-6; Deuteronomy 9:12-29; I Samuel 1:9-20; Joshua 10:12-14)

Jesus teaches that apart from prayer there is no spiritual life. He exemplified this through his own life and ministry in which he continuously kept in communion with the Father. Prayer is indispensable to our spiritual journey in which we seek to grow into the image of Christ. It is through prayer that we are forgiven, spiritually quickened, and receive the gifts of God. It is also prayer that provides the power to resist the temptations that lead people into sinful living. The Scriptures exhort us to call upon the Lord while he may be found, which means that one day all opportunities will cease. (Psalm 32:6; Isaiah 55:6)

God's mercy is promised to the pure in heart, who seek after righteousness. The apostle John affirms that God hears those who fear him and desire to do his will. (John 9:31) King David reassures us that the Lord's ears are attentive to the cries of the righteous, whom he delivers from their troubles. David wrote, "The Lord is near to all who call upon him, to all who call upon him in truth. He fulfills the desires of those who fear him; he hears their cries and saves them." (Psalm 145:18,19) Solomon wrote that the prayers of the upright who pursue righteousness please God. (Proverbs 15:8,9) The writer of Hebrews tells us that, even though Jesus is the Son of God, his prayers manifest reverent submission. (Hebrews 5:7)

The teachings of Jesus acknowledge that tribulation will come, but in him there is victory. (John 16:33; cp. John 5:4,5 and Romans 8:37) Whether it is trials directly related to sin or the afflictions that God allows to enter our lives, prayer opens the channel for sustaining grace and spiritual renewal. Paul's life reveals intense suffering, but through prayer he was assured of the Lord's continuing and all sufficient grace. Through all of his trials he never wavered in his faith, knowing that adversity provided opportunity to reveal God's presence and glory. Paul even used his incarceration to share the message of Christ. (Romans 8:35-37; II Corinthians 12:7-10)

The gospel is an invitation to be reconciled with God through the atoning grace of Jesus Christ, and the benefits of this relationship are realized through our prayer life. Prayer begins the sanctifying process through which we develop the divine nature, becoming one with Jesus in spirit and mission. As we prayerfully grow in Christ we begin to see life and relationships through his eyes, and this enables us to be witnesses of God's love and power.

Chapter One
Foundations for Prayer

God's people have always gathered for fellowship, worship, and prayer. Whether it was in the wilderness tabernacle, regional synagogues, the temple in Jerusalem, or the residences of early Christians, the Holy Spirit brings individuals together for mutual encouragement and support. After Jesus' ascension, his inner circle assembled in Jerusalem, and believers have been meeting since that time. (Acts 1:12-14) It is important that Christians meet together to share their joys and concerns, as well as participate in intercessory prayer. It is God's will that we be a priesthood of believers, reaching out to one another with concrete acts of love.

During his earthly ministry Jesus was an example of prayer for his followers. His disciples observed him praying on all occasions throughout his ministry. His prayers included praise and thanksgiving, as well as asking the Father for strength and guidance. Jesus also prayed for others, both the faithful and those living in sin. On a particular day the apostles witnessed an unusual display of his anger over the misuse of the temple in Jerusalem. In his anguish, Jesus told the people that God's temple is a house of prayer, not a commercial opportunity for greed, deception, and theft. (Luke 19:46) Prayer was fundamental to Jesus, a truth that he continuously communicated to others through teachings and example. His disciples soon realized that his inner strength and miraculous power came through his communion with the Father. This is certainly a lesson that needs to be emphasized in the Church. Rather than walking in the power of prayer, we too often rely upon our own wisdom and strength.

The Vine and Branches

Jesus' lesson on the *Vine and Branches* conveys graphic imagery of what occurs when people willfully separate themselves from him. As the One True Vine, he emphasizes the necessity to trust him for all of our needs. To separate ourselves from Christ is to reject his empowering and sustaining grace. However, to remain in Jesus through an active and meaningful prayer life implies intimacy. We must always seek to deepen our relationship with God, and this speaks directly to prayer. Just as branches depend upon the life of the vine, we cannot live and bear fruit apart from the life that is found in our Savior. Jesus said:

> I am the vine; you are the branches. If a man remains in me and I in him, he will bear much fruit; apart from me you can do nothing. If anyone does not remain in me, he is like a branch that is thrown away and withers; such branches are picked up, thrown into the fire and burned. If you remain in me and my words remain in you, ask whatever you wish, and it will be given to you. This is to my Father's glory, that

you bear much fruit, showing yourselves to be my disciples. (John 15:5-8)

This teaching, although troublesome for the non-Christian world, are the words that bring us forgiveness and eternal life in God's kingdom. As the True Vine, Jesus is the way to the Father, and those who remain in him will bear the fruit of the Spirit. (John 14:5,6) Such fruit includes the gifts needed for both personal transformation and ministry to others. When Jesus speaks about receiving what we ask for, he is primarily referring to the gifts that change one's inner life and spiritual walk. This is not to say that God fails to respond to other concerns and petitions.

Jesus told his listeners that he is the Bread of Life, emphasizing that he is our spiritual sustenance. He declared that those who come to him will never go hungry, nor will they thirst. (John 6:32-35) To walk in the teachings of Christ is to acknowledge him as our intercessor before the Father. Therefore, we must frequently and honestly examine our lives, praying for the faith and understanding that will enable us to assume the divine nature.

Marriage Analogy

Jesus compares our relationship with him as a marriage in which he is the bridegroom, and the Church is his bride. In Revelation we read, "Then I saw a new heaven and a new earth, for the first heaven and the first earth had passed away, and there was no longer any sea. I saw the Holy City, the new Jerusalem coming down out of heaven from God, prepared as a bride beautifully dressed for her husband." (Revelation 21:1,2) This passage, like the parable of the *Ten Virgins*, reflects Hebrew theological concepts to describe our relationship with the Lord. Just as the marriage to a spouse is rooted in love, faith, and commitment, it is nourished through sensitive and honest communications. Without the verbal exchange of thoughts, feelings, and needs, we may have a legal marriage, but not the relationship intended by God. This truth can also be applied to our spiritual life and relationship with Christ. Although we may proclaim discipleship, without communion with the Lord we are Christians in name only.

As both a pastor and counselor, I have worked with many couples who were experiencing difficulties in their marriage. While some of these relationships were plagued with complex and unresolved issues from the past, either from the family of origin or a previous marriage, it was the lack of communications that prevented healing and nurturing. It is so difficult for individuals to share with one another in a sensitive and caring way, looking beyond oneself to what the other person is experiencing. Many counseling sessions lead to increased stress as couples refuse to let go of the past.

In like manner, the failure to open our souls to the Lord and be sensitive to the Spirit's movement, is the barrier that prevents spiritual growth and maturity. It is difficult to trust God when you are not in communion with him, allowing the Spirit to address your innermost needs. Without the intimate relationship that comes through prayer, our spiritual lives are not only shallow, but we lose the assurance of a divine presence. There is no topic that is beyond the scope of prayer, for whatever matters to us, regardless how trivial it may seem, is a concern of God.

Knowing God's Will

Since the beginning of time the Lord has revealed himself to the humanity he created. Such manifestations have been realized through nature and miraculous signs, as well as through individual servants and the life of the Church. God is also made known through his Word and the compassionate acts of people. The Scriptures, particularly the teachings of the New Testament, enlighten us concerning God's will. But we are also encouraged to pray for the Lord's guidance and will, knowing that he has a personalized plan for each of us. Having said this, it is fortunate that we are not shown the distant future. If God were to disclose our entire road map and earthly journey we would be overwhelmed, with anxiety and self-will consuming us in destructive ways. Self-control would block the grace made possible through the movement of the Holy Spirit.

Our lives must prayerfully be given to the Lord, knowing that personal fulfillment and meaning are found in God's wisdom and timing. Through our surrender, the pieces of our life come together into a mosaic that fits God's plan for us. Rather than actively searching for God's will, our prayers are the channel through which the Lord unfolds his will for us. What occurs is a natural process in which our Creator is involved in every aspect of our lives. In other words, those who daily pray for God's will can end their search. All that matters is that we, in faith, accept the divine plan as it progresses. There is no reason to become anxious about the future or to look for momentous acts. People who are always looking to the future miss the blessings of the present. As the salt of the earth we are challenged to serve God where we are, leaving the future to the one who created us.

I was in my mid-thirties when I received Jesus Christ as my Savior. At that time, little thought was given to knowing God's will for my life. My first concern was to acquire the knowledge and understanding that would deepen my faith and understanding. Although I was not persistently praying for God's will at the time, the Lord was moving in my life. Little did I know that I would leave a law enforcement career for ordained ministry and eventually become a state prison chaplain. The key to God's will is personal surrender, which unquestionably involves prayer. However, even when I purposely sought direction, I had no insight into the future. Even now, as a retired pastor, the Lord continues to accomplish his will through my part-time ministries, speaking engagements, and writing. We can be assured that our prayers for divine leading will never go unanswered. If I had known the twists and turns that my life would take over the years, there would have been disbelief, anxiety, and possibly even fear. My early prayers for God's will were not seen within the context of being a pastor, but God had laid out a path before me that was unfolding without my knowledge. It was a path that combined study, along with various opportunities for ministry.

It is interesting to look back upon my life, realizing that it was a building process that even included my rebellious years. Sometimes we forget that through surrender and prayer God is able to use our entire life to his glory, including those dark times when we chose to travel a destructive path. Both our past sins and trials can be used to increase our compassion and understanding toward others who are living as we once did. Our identification with their temptations, weaknesses, and sins, can be an effective tool for a healing ministry that offers them a new life in Jesus Christ.

Praying for God's will is a serious matter, for it may take us down a difficult road. This is clearly exemplified with the life of Mary, the mother of Jesus. When the angel Gabriel announced to Mary that she would conceive through the power of the Holy

Spirit, she was shocked and afraid, not understanding why this was happening. But in her desire to do God's will she responded by saying, "I am the Lord's servant. May it be to me as you have said." (Luke 1:38) Little did Mary know that she would be the mother of our Savior, and that God's will for her son would be his sacrificial death for the sins of the world. In the Garden of Gethsemane Jesus prayed for the Father's will, knowing beforehand the agony that he would endure. Since then, countless Christians have suffered doing the will of God, giving their lives for a higher purpose. As we pray for God's leading, we must be willing to accept the answer we are given.

The Lord cares about the whole person, desiring to be involved in our daily living, and this is one reason why prayer is essential. We cannot compartmentalize our lives, separating the spiritual dimension from other activities and relationships. God is concerned about all that we do, and how it impacts upon his plan. Everything in life is interconnected and must involve God's presence and blessing. We are called to follow God's predestined path, which unfolds through prayer and surrender.

The Lord's Prayer

Prior to providing his disciples with the insights given in the Lord's Prayer, Jesus warned them about modeling themselves after hypocrites, whose prayers were theatrical performances aimed at seeking attention and the praise of people. He said, "When you pray, do not be like the hypocrites, for they love to pray standing in the synagogues and on the street corners to be seen by men. I tell you the truth, they have received their reward in full." (Matthew 6:5) Jesus used this brief lesson to assure his disciples that God knows our needs before we come to him in prayer. Therefore, unlike those who revel in their wordiness and theatrics, our prayers must not draw attention. He cautioned them against meaningless utterances that serve no purpose and were not from the heart. It was after this introductory teaching that Jesus shared the prayer that we have been reciting since childhood, using brevity to highlight the areas that we should prioritize in our communion with God.

As you will discover, the Lord's Prayer speaks to both our relationship with God and one another. It is interesting to note that this prayer addresses temptation and evil, subjects that are frequently found in Jesus' teachings and conversations with his apostles. These topics, however, are often absent in church ministries and personal prayer. Submission to sin has far reaching and recycling effects that extend beyond the present.

Hopefully, our brief examination of the Lord's Prayer will provide the understanding intended by Jesus. The text for this prayer is found in Matthew 6:9-14 and Luke 11:2-4.

Our Father in heaven, hallowed be your name
Just as Jesus prayed to the Father, he teaches us to do the same. In all of his prayers, our Savior addressed the first person of the Godhead as Father. This continued to the day of his death, when he called out to the Father in his suffering. Jesus committed his spirit to the Father while he was taking his last breath. After his resurrection, Jesus told Mary of Magdala that she should not attempt to hold on to his physical presence, that he must return to the Father. He said, "Do not hold on to me, for I have not yet returned to the Father. Go instead to my brothers, and tell them that I am returning to my Father and your Father, to my God and your God." (John 20:17) These and other scriptural references have established that God is our heavenly Father, and we are to approach him in this manner.

The attributes of a loving father are well known, but as our heavenly Father and Creator, God's love and protection are eternal. In this opening statement, Jesus wants us to know that God is the Father of all creation, and we are to acknowledge him as such. Regardless how difficult life becomes, we have a heavenly Father who watches over us. Like the biblical story of Job, the Lord is cognizant of our trials and suffering, and he will always provide comfort and strength. In the midst of his difficulties and pain, King David frequently wrote about God's delivering power; how the Lord was his strength, rock, and refuge.

The commencement of the Lord's Prayer also recognizes God as the absolute ruler of the universe, with his sovereignty and holiness undisputed. This statement is foundational to our beliefs, for it brings perspective to our lives. God is the Potter, and we are the clay. This means that we are totally dependent upon our Creator's mercy and sustaining grace. God's laws are perfect, his love is infinite and pure, and his power is beyond human comprehension. Although we exercise free will, it is God who oversees history and has the final word. In Revelation we read, "We give thanks to you, Lord God Almighty, who is and who was, because you have taken your power and have begun to reign." And again, "I heard what sounded like the roar of a great multitude in heaven shouting: Hallelujah! Salvation and glory and power belong to our God, for true and just are his judgments." (Revelation 11:17; 19:1,2) Only when we recognize and submit to God's absolute authority can we approach his throne in the humility, reverence, and faith that is required of us. Approaching the Lord in this spirit opens a channel for grace.

Your kingdom come, your will be done, on earth as it is in heaven
Praying for God's kingdom has both a present and an eschatological significance. While the Lord fulfills his will in the

heavenly places, we are called to build his earthly kingdom through prayer, witness, and by planting the seeds of God's forgiving grace through Jesus Christ. The Church represents the body of Christ, and this makes us kingdom builders. When pondering the meaning of our discipleship and the responsibility that comes with being a Christian, it is difficult to understand how people fail to see the weight of their influences and example. God has given us gifts to invest for him, and one day we will give an account of those investments.

Some people say that praying for an earthly kingdom is wishful thinking in a world of sin, where violence and wars take center stage. How can a spiritual kingdom be built in the midst of pride, prejudice, anger, and hatred? After all, history reveals that sin has always had the stronger influence over the human heart. Although no one would argue with the power of sin, nothing can overcome God's love and sovereignty. This is the same world that Jesus was born into, where his message was planted during a time of extreme oppression and violence. It is also where countless lives have been changed since the gospel was first preached. It is where Jesus called his first disciples, whose knowledge, faith, and mission, would be the beginning of an earthly kingdom that cannot be destroyed. Worldly kingdoms have come and gone, but the kingdom of God is eternal. It was amid violence and human bondage that Jesus came, with a message that would transform the darkest souls. Our prayers are not for a perfect world, but we are called to sow the seeds of God's love, and we are to pray for a harvest. God's Word has taken root during the worst of times, and it will continue to do so through our prayers. Those who come to Christ not only enter God's kingdom, but they become witnesses of his truth. Our obedience to the Lord will hasten the Second Advent of our Savior, when sin will be destroyed and holiness will reign.

Give us today our daily bread

The cliché *one day at a time*, which is a favorite expression amongst prison inmates, has some application here. Rather than being anxious about the future, God wants us to live in the present and to trust him for our future. If the Lord satisfies our present needs, then he will surely provide for our future. We tend to become fearful about the road ahead of us, when there is enough to be concerned about in the present. Jesus said to his disciples:

> Do not worry about your life, what you will eat or drink; or about your body, what you will wear. Is not life more important than food, and the body more important than clothes? Look at the birds of the air; they do not sow or reap or store away in barns, and yet your heavenly Father feeds them. Are you not much more valuable than they? Who of you by worrying can add a single hour to his life? And why do you worry about clothes? See how the lilies of the field grow. They do not labor or spin. Yet I tell you that not even Solomon in all his splendor was dressed like one of these. If that is how God clothes the grass of the field, which is here today and tomorrow is thrown into the fire, will he not much more clothe you, O you of little faith? (Matthew 6:25-30)

Jesus continued this discourse by assuring the apostles that God was aware of their needs. He emphasized that if the kingdom were their priority, all their needs would be met. He said, "Do not worry about tomorrow, for tomorrow will worry about itself. Each day has enough trouble of its own." (Matthew 6:31-34) We should note that Jesus was talking about needs and not human desires. Sometimes we confuse our desires with needs, and this distorts the truth that Jesus is conveying. To pray for our daily bread is to trust God for supplying our daily needs. It is also surrendering our future needs to his providence and will. This, of course, requires faith, which is an important part of this petition.

The apostles had to place their trust in Jesus for both their needs and those of their families. It is not clear what arrangements were made with their families, but we know that the apostles spent considerable time away from family members who undoubtedly depended upon them. Can you imagine placing yourself in the position of these men? I am certain that they had doubts, and that their trust in Jesus was a process that developed over time. For whatever period of time, it is difficult to imagine leaving family, friends, and employment, to follow an itinerant preacher whose ministry was always being questioned. This is not to mention the threats against their lives. On one occasion Peter was quick to remind Jesus of their situation when he said, "We have left everything to follow you! What then will there be for us?" (Matthew 19:27)

While our situation differs from the first disciples, we are nonetheless called to trust God for the necessities of life. Like the apostles, we must walk in faith each day, while resting in the Lord's promises for the future. As I share these truths with you, I am reminded again of my call to the ministry. I was in my thirties and a veteran law enforcement officer, who was moving up the supervision ladder. The idea of being a pastor was beyond my comprehension, and I resisted God's leading for two years. My thoughts focused upon my present position with its benefits and security, and the thought of college and seminary was inconceivable. My family and friends believed that I had either lost my mind, or was somehow being misled. Little did we know the plans that God had for me. And now, twenty-five years later, I cannot imagine taking another path in life. But the road was not easy, for there were certainly mistakes and obstacles along the way.

Jesus told his apostles to expect difficulties in this life, especially in light of the path that they were about to travel. They had to depend upon Jesus for their daily needs, which required trusting a man whom they did not always understand. They were certain, however, that his message spoke to their innermost needs. Jesus told them to take heart, that through him they would overcome the world. (John 16:33) He also promised them the Holy Spirit, who would bring them comfort and power, and when he commissioned the apostles he assured them of his abiding presence. (John 14:15,16; Matthew 28:20) The apostle John revealed trust in our Lord's words when he wrote to the Christians in Asia Minor, saying, "You, dear children, are from God and have overcome them, because the one who is in you is greater than the one who is in the world." (I John 4:4) The Scriptures promise that God will never leave or forsake us; that he will meet our daily needs. (Hebrews 13:5,6) When we call to the Lord for our daily bread, we are placing our faith in him for our present and continuing needs.

Forgive us our debts, as we also have forgiven our debtors

Without repentance and forgiveness there is no reconciliation with God, which means that forgiveness is necessary for salvation. While the Lord is the initiator of our salvation, we are called to respond in faith and with a penitent heart. Repentance is an attitude of the heart that brings inner cleansing through the power of the Holy Spirit. However, even though we have been changed, it does not mean that we are without sin. According to the apostle John, all wrongdoing is sin. In a letter to fellow Christians he said:

> If we claim to be without sin we deceive ourselves, and the truth is not in us. If we confess our sins, he is faithful and just and will forgive us our sins and purify us from all unrighteousness. If we claim we have not sinned, we make him out to be a liar, and his word has no place in our lives. (I John 1:8-10)

The mission of John the Baptist was to bring people back to God by preaching a message of repentance for the forgiveness of sins. John's ministry challenged people to look at the sin in their lives and how it was separating them from God and one another. His call to repent and be baptized as a sign of God's inner working of grace, was the foundation for the ministry of Jesus. John was our Savior's forerunner, who was preparing the hearts of people for the gospel message. After John was imprisoned by Herod, "Jesus came into Galilee proclaiming the good news of God. The time has come he said. The kingdom of God is near. Repent and believe the good news." (Mark 1:14,15) The good news, of course, is that Jesus came into the world to save us from sin and death.

These truths emphasize that our forgiveness comes through a humble and contrite heart. When in sorrow and faith, we confess our sins, seeking a relationship with Christ, we experience the spiritual birth that accompanies God's forgiveness. Through continuous self-examination and confession, we renew our spirits and take upon ourselves the nature and mission of Christ. God searches the inner life of every person, and he knows whether our hearts are pure. After King David committed adultery with Bathsheba and sent her husband Uriah into battle to assure his death, the prophet Nathan confronted him with his sins. In Psalm 51, David reveals the depth of his guilt as he confessed to God, saying:

> Have mercy on me, O God, according to your unfailing love; according to your great compassion, blot out my transgression. Wash away all my iniquity and cleanse me from my sin. For I know my transgressions, and my sin is always before me. Against you only have I sinned and done what is evil in your sight. Let me hear joy and gladness; let the bones you have crushed rejoice. Hide your face from my sins, and blot out all my iniquity. Create in me a pure heart, 0 God, and renew a steadfast spirit within me. Do not cast me away from your presence, or take your Holy Spirit from me. Restore to me the joy of your salvation, and grant me a willing spirit to sustain me. The sacrifices of God are a broken spirit, a broken and contrite heart. (Psalm 51:1-4,8-12,17)

David not only felt the overwhelming weight of his sins, but he knew that there was no salvation without God's forgiveness. In verse eleven David prayed for restoration and the continued presence of the Holy Spirit. David's sins were grievous, and it wasn't long before they would have personal results and take their toll upon others. But all sin is against God and needs continuing forgiveness. While we recognize the transformation that takes place through God's grace, there will always be the need for forgiveness in this life. The Lord's Prayer may be brief in content, but it accentuates this ongoing necessity.

While forgiveness is normally understood as a personal matter, it must also be viewed within the context of Christian congregations and the universal Church. Since its inception, the Church has committed many sins, including sins of omission when Christians should have taken an active part in confronting evil. In recent years the Church has openly repented of some past sins, which has had a cleansing effect and may serve to guard against future sins. While Jesus certainly confronted individuals with their need to repent, he addressed the larger Church as well. Through divine inspiration the apostle John warned the congregation in Ephesus, saying, "You have forsaken your first love. Remember the height from which you have fallen! Repent and do the things you did at first. If you do not repent, I will come to you and remove your lampstand from its place." (Revelation 2:4,5) These words reveal that the wider Church is being scrutinized by God and will be judged for losing its way. In his lesson of an unproductive fig tree that is about to be cut down for its lack of fruit, Jesus reveals that God will judge nations that do not produce spiritual fruit. (Luke 13:6-8)

Both individuals and nations are to seek the Lord while there is opportunity. Isaiah's words are timeless when he said, "Seek the Lord while he may be found; call on him while he is near. Let the wicked forsake his way, and the evil man his thoughts. Let him turn to the Lord, and he will have mercy on him, and to our God, for he will freely pardon." (Isaiah 55:6,7) God told Israel that he would forgive their sins and remember them no more, and here lies the good news offered by Jesus. (Isaiah 43:25) The angel told Joseph and Mary that their son would save the people from their sins. This forgiving grace was the fulfillment of Hebrew prophecy and the hope of the world. Jesus' reference to himself as the Son of Man, found eighty-two times in the New Testament, was his claim to be the Messiah promised by God. The prophet Daniel experienced an apocalyptic vision in which he saw, "one like a son of man coming on the clouds of heaven." Daniel wrote that this man "approached the Ancient of Days and was led into his presence. He was given authority, glory, and sovereign power; all peoples, nations, and men of every language worshipped him. His dominion is an everlasting dominion that will not pass away, and his kingdom is one that will never be destroyed." (Daniel 7:13,14) The Book of Enoch communicated a similar image, with an emphasis upon a universal judgment. (Enoch 46:1-6; 48:2-10; 62:5-16; 63:11; 69:26-29; 70:1) Although there are other Messianic scriptures in the Hebrew Bible, as early as Genesis 3:15, the passage in the Book of Daniel was well know to the Jews, who were anxiously awaiting God's Anointed One.

Forgiveness is at the heart of the incarnation and the sacrificial death of Jesus. It is the central message of the gospel and the means through which we receive eternal life. The apostle Peter said to a crowd, "This is how God fulfilled what he had foretold through the prophets, saying that his Christ would suffer. Repent, then, and turn to God, so that your sins may be wiped out, that times of refreshing may come from the Lord, and that he may send the Christ, who has been appointed for you—even Jesus." (Acts 3:19,20) Peter repeatedly urged the people to repent and be baptized in the name of Jesus, that their sins might be forgiven. (Acts 2:38)

Whether it is sinful thoughts, words, or actions, there is the need to confess our sins and to seek the forgiveness that brings inner cleansing. We must also address sins of omission, including those relating to spiritual complacency and laziness. These are the sins that stifle our growth and prevent others from receiving God's grace through us. The Lord has placed each of us in a position of responsibility, meaning that our gifts are to be used for God's glory. This is accomplished when we use our gifts for the benefit of other people, especially those who are in need.

The Scriptures teach us that we are the keepers of our brothers and sisters; therefore, we are sent out to the less fortunate. We are answerable to God as individuals and as a Church and nation. Toward the end of his ministry Jesus posed a question to Peter. Three times he asked Peter if he loved him, and Peter responded yes each time. Jesus then told Peter to feed and take care of his sheep. Peter became a leader in the Church, charged with overseeing the spreading of the gospel, as well as meeting the needs of the people. This is the ministry that has been given to every Christian. (John 12:15-17)

In the Lord's Prayer we not only seek the forgiveness of our sins, but we acknowledge our willingness to forgive others. Many people fail to see the connection between these dual aspects of forgiveness. Actually, the two are inseparable, for our forgiveness hinges upon our pardon of other people. It is easy to say that we forgive someone, but a search of the heart often reveals a refusal to put the past behind us. The ability to forgive an offense is a spiritual matter that requires earnest desire and persistent communion with God.

Depending upon the offense, it may be difficult to forgive another person, particularly when a violent crime is involved. But through prayer the Holy Spirit begins the forgiving process. Although we may not forget the sin, the Lord removes the pain that accompanies bitterness and anger. This provides an inner peace that facilitates spiritual healing and renewal. The failure to forgive has a personal cost, because it robs us of the sanctifying grace that deepens our relationship with the Lord. An unforgiving heart lacks the purity that is needed to commune with God, thereby damaging the peace and transforming benefits that the Lord offers us. Paul touched upon this in a letter written to fellow Christians. He said:

Do not grieve the Holy Spirit of God, with whom you were sealed for the day of redemption. Get rid of all bitterness, rage and anger, brawling and slander. Be kind and compassionate to one another, forgiving each other, just as in Christ God forgave you. (Ephesians 4:30-32)

Jesus told his disciples, "When you stand praying, if you hold anything against anyone, forgive him, so that your Father in heaven may forgive you your sins." (Mark 11:25) Some manuscripts read, "But if you do not forgive, neither will your Father who is in heaven forgive your transgressions." (New American Standard and King James versions) There are biblical passages that are difficult to translate, but these verses are clearly stated and not open to another interpretation.

In the parable of the *Unmerciful Servant*, Jesus tells us about a king who wanted to settle accounts with his servants. One servant, who owed the king ten thousand talents, was unable to pay his debt. As a result, the king ordered that he, his family, and all that he owned be sold to satisfy what was owed. But the servant fell on his knees, begging his master for mercy. The king took pity on him, and in an act of kindness he canceled the entire debt. This, however, is not the end of the story, for this same servant had a fellow servant who owed him money. He demanded that the man pay him, even becoming violent by grabbing and choking him. The man begged for mercy, but it did not change the situation. He was thrown into prison until the debt could be satisfied. When the other servants heard what had transpired they reported the incident to their master, who immediately called this unmerciful servant before him, saying:

You wicked servant, I canceled all that debt of yours because you begged me to. Shouldn't you have had mercy on your fellow servant just as I had mercy on you? In his anger his master turned him over to the jailers until he should pay back all he owed. This is how my heavenly Father will treat each of you unless you forgive your brother from the heart. (Matthew 18:32-35)

This graphic story resulted from a question that Peter had posed to Jesus. He asked, "How many times should I forgive my brother when he sins against me? Up to seven times?" Jesus told Peter that he should forgive others seventy-seven times. (Matthew 18:21,22) Ancient Jewish rabbis taught that a person should forgive another person three times, but not the fourth. Peter more than doubled this, believing himself to be generous. Little did he know the answer that Jesus would give him. Like many people today, he failed to understand the meaning and depth of forgiveness. Can you imagine the peace and spiritual growth that people would experience if they walked in the spirit of forgiveness?

The Scriptures speak about an incident in which the teachers of the law and the Pharisees brought a woman to Jesus who was caught in the act of adultery. They said, "In the Law Moses commanded us to stone such a woman. Now what do you say?" Jesus' immediate response was to bend down and write something in the ground with his finger. When the woman's accusers continued to question him, Jesus said, "If any one of you is without sin, let him be the first to throw a stone at her." With this response the men departed, with the older ones leaving first.(John 8:1-11)

Jesus forgave the woman of a crime that was punishable by

death, showing compassion when the law dictated otherwise. Rather than be someone's judge and jury, condemning them as an outcast, his love and forgiveness gave her a new beginning. People tend to lay down ground rules when it comes to forgiveness, but if the Lord were to do this with us, we would never experience his love and salvation. Instead of condemning the woman caught in adultery, Jesus told her to live a righteous life.

Is forgetting a necessary part of forgiveness? In other words, can we forget the things that people do to us? Although this may be debated, I doubt that even the most spiritual individuals forget certain offenses. But as previously stated, it is desire and a pure heart that moves us down the path of forgiveness. Through continuous prayer there is less thought given to the negative behavior of other people. In fact, when we begin praying for the other person's transformation and spiritual life, we rid ourselves of the animosity that has a grip on us. The apostle Peter, in following the teachings of Christ, states that we must never repay evil with evil or insult with insult. Instead, we should pray about these situations and find some way to reach out to those who persecute us, for this is the Lord's will. (I Peter 3:9)

The teachings and passion of Christ provide the ultimate example of forgiveness. Like our Savior, we are to forgive our enemies and pray for those who persecute us. In preaching to a large crowd, Jesus said:

> But I tell you who hear me: Love your enemies, do good to those who hate you. Bless those who curse you, pray for those who mistreat you. If someone takes your cloak, do not stop him from taking your tunic. Give to anyone who asks you, and if anyone

> takes what belongs to you, do not demand it back.
> Do to others as you would have them do to you. If
> you love those who love you, what credit is that to
> you? Even sinners love those who love them. But
> love your enemies, do good to them, and lend to
> them without expecting to get anything back. Then
> your reward will be great, and you will be sons of the
> Most High, because he is kind to the ungrateful and
> wicked. Be merciful, just as your Father is merciful.
> (Luke 6:27-32,35,36)

This was, and continues to be a radical teaching, even for Christians. In this lesson Jesus redefines our relationships, placing them within the context of humility and self-sacrifice. What we find here is the divine nature of Jesus Christ, which he desires to instill in us. His suffering and death is for all sinners, including those who have committed heinous crimes. He gave his life so that everyone who receives him might be forgiven and have the fullness of God's grace.

My ministries have revealed that few people think about their need to forgive one another. Rather than pray for a forgiving heart, people tend to justify their bitterness and anger. Somehow, it is always the other person's fault, and it is they who must take the initiative to make amends. The biblical teaching that forgiveness is directly related to our salvation is seldom communicated in Christian circles. Even those who have a viable prayer life tend to fall short in this area. The Church also shares in this failure by not emphasizing the dual aspects of forgiveness. These realities, along with negative family and secular influences, combine to paint a troublesome picture when it comes to forgiving others.

Lead us not into temptation

Regardless of one's spiritual knowledge and maturity, we will always be confronted with temptation. They include both the obvious influences, as well as the subtle and latent forces that seek our destruction. People seem oblivious to life's many seductions, unless they are blatant and disrupt their life. Alcoholism, drug addiction, adultery, and criminal violations, typically fall into this category. Seldom is thought given to those subtle temptations that lead to sin. Jesus tells us that sin begins in the heart, where all evil acts have their roots. Concerning adultery, Jesus said, "You have heard that it was said do not commit adultery. But I tell you that anyone who looks at a woman lustfully has already committed adultery with her in his heart." (Matthew 5:27,28) Jesus continued this teaching by saying, "If your right eye causes you to sin, gouge it out and throw it away. It is better for you to lose one part of your body than for your whole body to be thrown into hell." (verse 29) The latter passage is a hyperbolic statement to emphasize that we must be aggressive in resisting evil. Jesus often used exaggerated and figurative language to get his listener's attention and to reinforce a truth. This teaching technique reveals the extent of evil in the world and its power over people.

The apostle Paul warned the Ephesians, "Our struggle is not against flesh and blood, but against the rulers, against the authorities, against the powers of this dark world and against the spiritual forces of evil in the heavenly realm." (Ephesians 6:12) Fighting evil temptations requires the full armor of God, which includes faith and prayer. (verses 13-20) This means that fighting temptation requires a power higher than ourselves; therefore, we must resist pride and self-will, and come to the Lord for the strength that we need.

No one understands the power of temptation more than our Savior, who was relentlessly attacked by Satan during his forty days in the desert. It was in this wilderness setting that Jesus fasted and prayed in preparation for his ministry and ultimate sacrifice. During this time Satan was unyielding in his assaults, striking at every human weakness in an attempt to derail God's mission to the lost and dying. Jesus answered the attacks in faith and with the power of God's Word. As a result, the devil left Jesus, waiting for another opportunity. (Matthew 4:1-11)

This tells us that we must be grounded in the Word, faithfully standing upon God's promises. Peter wrote that the Lord will deliver the righteous from temptation, and the apostle James assures us that the devil will flee from those who resist him. (II Peter 2:9; James 4:7) We must make every effort not to place ourselves in the path of temptation, knowing that the daily influences of life are difficult enough to confront. In his wisdom, King Solomon exhorts us to disassociate ourselves from those bent upon doing evil, that we not be tempted. In Proverbs he wrote, "Do not set foot on the path of the wicked or walk in the way of evil men. Avoid it, do not travel on it; turn from it and go your own way. Can a man scoop fire into his lap without his clothes being burned? Can a man walk on hot coals without his feet being scorched?" (Proverbs 4:14,15; 6:27,28) Much of our temptation is self-inflicted through the associates and activities that we choose. It's like a recovering alcoholic who frequents taverns, believing there is no longer a threat.

Jesus' wilderness experience reveals that no one is beyond the influences and power of temptation. If Jesus was tempted, and the devil left him only to wait for another opportunity, then the message to us is clear. The existence of evil tells us that we will never be released from temptation. In fact, bringing down Christians and their leaders are certainly priorities for Satan. To damage the witness of the Church is the primary mission of the devil, for it is through the ministries of the Church that the world hears the gospel, looks for an example, and has opportunities for spiritual formation. It is the Church that brings the message of our Savior's victory. The writer of Hebrews addressed Jewish Christians by telling them that in Jesus Christ we have a high priest who was tempted in every way and can sympathize with our weaknesses. Therefore, we can approach God's throne of grace with confidence, knowing that in Christ there is understanding and help in our time of need. (Hebrews 4:15,16)

Paul told the Corinthian congregation that their temptations were common to everyone, and that God would not allow them to be tempted beyond what they could bear. He left no doubt that God would provide a way out of temptation, enabling them to stand firm. (I Corinthians 10:13) With similar words of encouragement, the apostle John tells us that the power of God in us is our victory. (I John 4:4) Some individuals attribute to Satan a power that is equal to God, which is the message that the devil strives to convey. We must never forget that God is the creator, sustainer, and judge of the universe, and that all power and glory belongs to him. Satan may tempt us, but he cannot force us to sin.

The world that Jesus entered and was sent to redeem was submitting to all manner of sin, and it continues today. The Lord knows our weaknesses, and he beseeches us to continuously pray for the power to resist sin. Just before his arrest he warned his apostles, saying, "Watch and pray so that you will not fall into temptation. The spirit is willing, but the body is weak." (Matthew 26:41) Like many areas in life, we often see temptation in terms of others rather than ourselves. Even when temptation is obvious, we believe that we have the power to resist. But as we ponder history, some of the most gifted and influential people in the world have been brought down by temptations relating to pride, power, greed, and lust.

Understanding life's temptations is complex, for it involves both external and internal forces that lead us away from biblical truths. Whether it is sinful desires, activities that consume our time, or the company that we keep, we live in a world of negative forces. Regardless where we are in our spiritual journey, the struggles and trials remain. Even though the desire of our hearts have changed, we will always experience negative influences. This spiritual battle, however, can be kept in check through prayer and God's sustaining and empowering grace. Jesus knew that his followers would be confronted with all manner of temptation, and this is why he emphasized the need for continuous prayer.

Deliver us from the evil one

This petition specifically speaks to the existence of Satan, a truth that some people in the Church deny. In the Lord's Prayer we are asking God for the grace to keep us from the control of Satan and demonic powers. The Scriptures teach us that Satan is the source of human pride and personal evil. It was Satan who was instrumental in the fall of humanity, resulting in our tarnished nature. Both the Hebrew Bible and the New Testament teach this truth. Beginning with the Book of Genesis we learn of Satan's existence and mission, and the story of Job contains graphic lessons on good and evil. The teachings of Jesus have created a doctrine of Satan that was continued by the apostles, early Church, and orthodox Christianity throughout the ages. You cannot read the Scriptures and disregard these passages. Paul was aware of Satan's existence, not only from his theological education, but also from his own experiences. He urged the church in Ephesus to trust in God's grace, that they might stand firm against the schemes of the devil. (Ephesians 6:11) But just as in Paul's day, these words continue to fall upon deaf ears. Even today, some professing Christians refuse to believe in these scriptural truths. If Satan does not exist, why did Jesus and the apostles fill their teachings and writings with this reality? Also, why did our Savior use the words, *deliver us from the evil one,* in this petition of the Lord's Prayer? But the debate in denominations and churches continues, with many individuals convinced that the word *Satan* is merely a symbol for evil.

This issue is compounded by today's emphasis upon the physical and material world. As we become increasingly secular, we move away from biblical truths and spiritual sensitivity. What the early Church possessed, has to some extent, been lost over the years in which technology, entertainment, and activities take precedence in our lives. In some congregations the teachings of Christ become less pertinent as people grapple with building funds and committee issues. It is not unusual for church leaders to discuss everything but spiritual matters. Regardless how progressive a church may be, the doctrine of Satan is seldom communicated. This is particularly true when influential members are opposed to such teachings.

The belief in Satan is taught in the Hebrew Bible and by every New Testament writer. These combined writings paint a clear picture of his personality and nature. The prophet Ezekiel wrote that the devil was an angelic being who fell from God's grace. (Ezekiel 28:11-19) Beginning with the Genesis account, Satan's rebellious pride has penetrated humanity with devastating results. Like an arsonist who sets a fire and watches the destruction, the devil has lit the flames of pride, rebellion, and hatred. God's inspired writers have given many names to Satan, including liar, murderer, adversary, and confirmed sinner and accuser of the saints. (John 8:44; I Peter 5:8; I John 3:8; Revelation 12:10) Paul called Satan the tempter, god of this age, prince of the power of the air, and the angel of light. (I Thessalonians 3:5; II Corinthians 4:4; Ephesians 2:2; II Corinthians 11:14) In Revelation, the apostle John refers to Satan as the serpent and dragon. (Revelation 12:3,9) These descriptive names given to Satan correspond with his personality and evil intent.

Satan was the first sinner, and Paul reveals that his sin was pride, which is the essence of all sin. Pride opens the door to disobedience and all manner of sin. When the devil fell from grace he took an angelic force with him. In the Garden of Eden he concealed himself in the serpent, mingling truth with falsehood. He persuaded Eve to disbelieve God, convincing her that she would not die for her actions. He aroused doubt in Eve's mind, and this same doubt exists with people today. (Genesis 3)

Satan's weapons, although disguised, have not changed since that encounter in the garden. He is the master of deception, and he employs his art at our weak moments. As the angel of light he imitates God, disguising his works of evil. He tries to convince us that he has our welfare in mind. Although Satan is not infinite or omnipotent, he has spread the seeds of pride, self-will, prejudice, and hatred, and they have recycled from one generation to another. His grand design is to destroy the kingdom of God within us, which includes attacking our spiritual sensitivity and development. He does this by pointing out our imperfections and sins, accentuating that we are beyond forgiveness and that holiness is unattainable. Satan also plants doubt concerning our faith, particularly during times of trial, when he tries to convince us that faith is simply an abstract concept that cannot bring divine power or salvation.

The devil additionally implants thoughts concerning death, trying to convince us that there is no life beyond the grave. This message encourages people to self-indulge in sinful ways, often at the cost to others. If life is not eternal and there is no accountability, then the door to evil and violence is wide open. As a police detective I had the opportunity of interviewing many murder suspects. When the question of accountability and God's judgment was raised, there was never much of a response. In fact, seldom did these individuals give thought to how their actions impacted upon others. This was also true during my tenure as a state prison chaplain. Although there are exceptions, the focus of many prisoners is upon themselves, rather than the pain that they caused their victims and their own families.

We should note that Satan attacks our strengths, as well as our weaknesses. It is easy to comprehend the latter, but seldom do we think about our strengths as being objects of assault. Everyone has gifts that can be used either for good or evil purposes. Our prisons are full of talented individuals who could be an asset to society if they applied their gifts for the good of others. The prison system incarcerates many professional people, including theologians, lawyers, artists, computer engineers, musicians, and accountants. While most inmates lack a formal education, many are self-educated, creative, or simply have potential. Unfortunately, these individuals have chosen to use their talents to the detriment of others.

In our prayers for deliverance from evil, we are asking God to protect us from Satan's control. Although we will always be subjected to temptation, being controlled by evil is quite different. Even in the penal system one realizes these distinctions. For example, there is a difference between someone who chooses a criminal lifestyle because of greed, as opposed to individuals whose desires are pure evil. The intensity of evil in some people affirms what the Scriptures teach, and to deny this is to reject God's Word. I spent many hours counseling inmates who shared their evil desires, believing that they were being controlled by an unseen force. Some of them thought that this control was of a demonic nature, and having been in their presence I did not doubt the possibility.

Satan's attacks on Christian morality and responsibility affect every area of life and segment of society. Whether it is unethical business practices, deceptive politicians, sexual immorality, or strife within the family, the existence of sin is real. Jesus knew the power of evil, for he was subjected to personal attacks during his entire ministry. The one who came preaching love and forgiveness, was confronted with every manner of demonic presence. The attacks that began in the wilderness continued at Golgatha, where he sacrificed his life for the darkness that had overcome the world. Like Jesus, we must clothe ourselves with God's Word, leaving no part of our lives vulnerable to evil.

Regardless of life's trials and the power of Satan, we are on the side of victory. Paul wrote that all of life's difficulties serve a higher purpose for those who love and serve the Lord. He said, "If God is for us, who can be against us?" Paul was convinced that nothing can overcome the faithful, who seek God's strength and guidance. He assured Christians that in Jesus Christ they were more than conquerors, meaning that their trials would serve to increase their faith and make them stronger. Their struggles would also enable them to be more understanding toward those who were experiencing difficulties. Paul told the church in Rome that nothing in all creation could separate them from the love of God that is found in Jesus Christ. (Romans 8:28-39)

For yours is the kingdom and the power and the glory forever

This acknowledgment was added to the Lord's Prayer at a later time. It is a declaration that yields all power and glory to our Creator, recognizing his eternal sovereignty and providence. After the ark of God was brought to Jerusalem, King David offered up a psalm in which he praised the Lord for his power and glory. It reads:

> Sing to the Lord all the earth, proclaim his salvation day after day. Declare his glory among the nations, his marvelous deeds among all the peoples. For great is the Lord and most worthy of praise; he is to be feared above all gods. For all the gods of the nations are idols, but the Lord made the heavens. Splendor and majesty are before him; strength and joy is his dwelling place. Ascribe to the Lord, O families of nations; ascribe to the Lord the glory due his name. Tremble before him all the earth. (I Chronicles 16:23-30)

Biblical history reveals the importance of offering up our praise and thanksgiving to the Lord. The Scriptures provide numerous examples when people of faith were moved to glorify God through written expressions and worship. In the Psalms, David and other writers are known for their worshipful praise. The ancients recognized the power and love of God in their lives, and they did not hesitate in making it known. A psalm sung by the Sons of Korah begins with the words, "Great is the Lord and most worthy of praise, in the city of our God, his holy mountain." (Psalm 48:1) These same writers penned the following tribute:

> Clap your hands, all you nations; shout to God with cries of joy. How awesome is the Lord Most High, the great King over all the earth! He subdued nations under us, peoples under our feet. He chose our inheritance for us, the pride of Jacob, whom he loved. (Psalm 47:1-4)

The Israelites praised God for his abiding presence and sustaining grace, how he brought them out of Egypt and provided for them in the desert. They sang the Lord's praises for victory over their enemies, and for the promises that he made to their forefathers, Abraham, Isaac, and Jacob. Isaiah wrote, "O Lord, you are my God; I will exalt you and praise your name, for in perfect faithfulness you have done marvelous things, planned long ago." (Isaiah 25:1) An unknown psalmnist glorified God with the following praise:

> Give thanks to the Lord, call on his name; make known among the nations what he has done. Sing to him, sing praises to him; tell of all his wonderful acts. Glory in his holy name, let the hearts of those who seek the Lord rejoice. Look to the Lord and his strength, seek his face always. Remember the wonders he has done, his miracles and the judgments he pronounces. (Psalm 105:1-5)

The prophet Jeremiah reminded the people of God's creative power, saying, "God made the earth by his power; he founded the world by his wisdom and stretched out the heavens by his understanding." (Jeremiah 10:12) Such themes are repeated by the prophets in an attempt to reveal God's glory to the people, and these same heart offerings are given by the New Testament writers. Peter told his readers, "If anyone serves, he should do it with the strength God provides, so that in all things God may be praised through Jesus Christ." (I Peter 4:11) Peter urges us to praise God through both our body and spirit, that our entire being would be an example of praise. This corresponds with Paul's words to the congregations in Rome and Corinth. (Romans 12:1,2; I Corinthians 6:19,20)

We praise God for his holiness, faithfulness, and for the mercy that emanates from his perfect love. When we acknowledge God's absolute sovereignty and our total dependence upon his grace, we become filled with praise and thanksgiving. As the clay in the Potter's hands we are molded and given life. The Lord rules the heart's of believers, and he is the final judge of humanity, rewarding the righteous with his eternal kingdom. Peter assures us that God has the power to keep us until the day when his glory is revealed. (I Peter 1:5) Paul wrote the church in Corinth that the God who had the power to raise Jesus from the dead has the same power to raise us. (I Corinthians 6:14) Acknowledging God's power and glory not only gives life perspective, but it also provides a channel for the fullness of divine grace.

++

Hopefully, the preceding insights have provided some understanding into the Lord's Prayer, and why Jesus shared this model with his apostles. Without this example many people would neglect these important petitions, which provide the foundation for understanding, inner strength, and personal development. The repetition of any prayer can become mundane and shallow over time; therefore, one must exercise spiritual discipline when citing each part of this prayer. This involves taking time to reflect upon the meaning and how it applies to your life. When we pray slowly, reflecting upon the words, we find ourselves in the presence of the Lord. To treat this prayer as simply a part of church liturgy or tradition, is to miss the understanding and blessings intended by God. As with the apostles, the Lord's Prayer is where our communion with God begins.

Intercession of the Holy Spirit

The apostle Paul wrote, "The Spirit helps us in our weaknesses. We do not know what we ought to pray, but the Spirit himself intercedes for us with groans that words cannot express. And he who searches our hearts knows the mind of the Spirit, because the Spirit intercedes for the saints in accordance with God's will." (Romans 8:26,27) The Holy Spirit has a crucial role in our prayer life, that of translating our burdens and concerns, and bringing them before God's throne of grace. While Christ makes intercession in his place of exaltation in the presence of God, the Spirit makes intercession from within the lives of believers. Our deep burdens and groans, which cannot be put into words, are translated by the Holy Spirit and offered up to the Lord. In Tyndale's Commentary of Paul's Epistle to the Romans, F.F. Bruce quotes James Montgomery, who caught the apostle's meaning, when he wrote:

> Prayer is the soul's sincere desire
> Uttered or unexpressed,
> The motion of a hidden fire
> That trembles in the breast.
> Prayer is the burden of a sigh,
> The falling of a tear,
> The upward glancing of an eye,
> When none but God is near. (p. 175)

The Holy Spirit, whose mind is read by the Father, takes our emotions, pain, and inarticulate feelings, and he intercedes for us before the throne of grace. Our weaknesses and lack of wisdom often prevent us from knowing how to pray. We cannot see into the future, nor do we know what is best for ourselves or other people. We come before the Lord with incoherent sighs emanating from the heart, which only the Holy Spirit can understand. The Greek philosopher Pythagoras (540-500 B.C.), who believed in the transmigration of the soul, forbade his disciples from praying for themselves. He believed that their ignorance prevented them from knowing what was in their best interest. While we are certainly told to pray, it is true that perfect wisdom and understanding belongs to God, and this speaks to the ministry of the Holy Spirit in our prayer life. Our thoughts and verbal expressions are not always aligned with our true feelings and needs, but the Spirit knows both our hearts and the Father's will. Like a mother who understands the sounds of her infant child, the Holy Spirit knows the meaning of our sighs, as well as our inability to express ourselves. This is particularly true during times of deep emotion and pain.

In addition to the intercessory work of the Holy Spirit, the epistles of Paul and Jude speak about our need to pray in the Spirit. Paul said that we should pray in the Spirit on all occasions with all kinds of prayer. (Ephesians 6:16; cp. Jude 20) But what does it means to pray in the Spirit? Are the ancients alluding to some manner of spiritual discipline that has become lost over the centuries? While there are varying interpretations of these passages, it is reasonable to conclude that those who live in Christ, lean upon the Holy Spirit's guidance as they come to the Lord in prayer. This, of course, means praying in faith. To the Galatians Paul said, "Did you receive the Spirit by observing the law, or by believing what you have heard? Are you so foolish? After beginning with the Spirit, are you now trying to attain your goal by human effort?" (Romans 8:9; Galatians 3:2,24; 5:18)

To pray in the Spirit is when, in humility and faith, we seek the heart and mind of Jesus Christ. By doing this we identify with the love and mission of our Savior, with the content of our prayers reflecting this. It means that our petitions will mirror that of a servant. As we take up the cross of love and self-sacrifice, walking in our Savior's footsteps, we become one with him in nature and mission. We are to offer ourselves up as living sacrifices that are holy and pleasing to the Lord. (Romans 12:1,2) In other words, praying in the Spirit becomes a reality as we assume the image of Christ.

The Lord has a plan for everyone, and it unfolds as we open up our hearts to him. Many people pray for worldly things, but Jesus tells us to make the kingdom of God our priority. (Matthew 6:33) Christians struggle maintaining this focus, allowing the distractions of secularism to consume them. Rather than praying for the spiritual gifts that change our inner life, thereby equipping us to be a priesthood of believers, we often ask for gifts that are outside of God's will. When praying, we should first seek the Spirit's presence and leading, and then reflect upon this request as we commune with God.

++

This chapter addressed the foundations for prayer that are found in both the Hebrew Bible and the New Testament. We examined two relational illustrations given by Jesus and how they speak to our salvation and spiritual development. The *Vine and Branches* and the *Spiritual Marriage* are graphic teachings, emphasizing the necessity of a personal relationship with Jesus Christ that is nurtured through faith and prayer. We also looked at the *Lord's Prayer*, which speaks to crucial areas for spiritual growth and maturity. Jesus gave this prayer to his disciples as an example of how they should approach God. Besides the acknowledgments of God's holiness, sovereignty, and glory, it focuses upon issues of faith, temptation, forgiveness, and evil.

Next, we learned that we are to align ourselves with God's will, realizing that it unfolds naturally as we walk in faith and prayerfully seek divine leading. Living in God's will enables his plan for us to unfold, making it possible to become servants of mercy.

We concluded this chapter with insights into the work of the Holy Spirit. As the divine resident and communicator of the heart, the Spirit moves through our emotions and thoughts, bringing our true feelings and concerns before the Lord. It is assuring to know that we have a perfect interpreter and advocate who is always there for us, especially during life's trials. We also learned the importance of praying in the Spirit, which occurs when we seek the Spirit's leading, as well as the heart and mind of Jesus. When we pray for the gifts of God, those relating to our spiritual journey and ministry to others, we experience the movement of the Spirit within us.

Chapter Two
Approaching God

The Struggle

Prayer can be a struggle during times of trial, and some people have more than their share of pain and loss. When our needs are most acute we sometimes have difficulty expressing ourselves to the Lord. In fact, people report dry periods when life's pressures affect their desire, energy, and ability to pray. These are often times of intense spiritual warfare, when submission to defeat seems to be the only path to take. When we need to pray the most, we often find the well going dry. Whether it is wavering faith or emotional upset, lacking the will to pray must be confronted by standing firm upon God's Word and promises. We must remember that our prayer life is not based upon how we feel, but rather upon God's love and his promise to never leave or forsake us.

Pastors attest to having periods when they have neglected their prayer life. Personal issues and needs within the parish take their toll on many pastors. Sometimes parishioners forget that their pastor is flesh and blood, subject to both family problems, as well as the needs within their congregations. Their stress is compounded by church issues that cannot be resolved, regardless how much time and energy is expended. During these times we must remember that God is in the midst of our struggles. Biblical writers repeatedly bear witness to God's never failing presence. King David, who knew the pain associated with trials, realized that strength was found in prayer and words of praise. In one of his psalms we read, "God is our refuge and strength, an ever present help in trouble. Therefore, we will not fear, though the earth gives way and the mountains fall into the sea." (Psalm 46:1; cp. Deuteronomy 31:6)

Jesus, who knew the agony of life, was aware of the adversity that awaited his disciples. In his commission to them, he promised his abiding presence. (Matthew 28:20) With the anticipation of his departure, he also assured them of God's presence when he said, "If you love me, you will obey what I command. And I will ask the Father, and he will give you another Counselor to be with you forever—the Spirit of truth." (John 14:15-17) In this life it is the Holy Spirit who provides comfort, strength, discernment, and leading. Although we are not removed from life's difficulties, it is the Spirit of truth who addresses our needs and keeps us on the righteous path. This is realized as we open our hearts to God in prayer, seeking his spiritual gifts through our surrendered life.

In Jesus Christ we have a Savior who completely identifies with our struggles, both the agony of the soul and the pain of the body. There is no temptation or trial that he did not endure. Jesus knows the feelings of being misunderstood, forsaken, and hated by others. The one who was sinless, falsely accused and crucified, knew the extreme abuses of humanity. But in the midst of his torture he prayed with absolute faith, trusting in the Father's presence, even when that presence was not experienced. This is a clear lesson for us, for we also are to trust God when the feelings are absent. During our hardships we must fight our doubt and approach God's throne in surrendered faith, trusting in his mercy, wisdom, and strength. Our understanding is limited, but the Lord's knowledge and wisdom is perfect.

The suffering of Jesus is forever a part of his divinity, and it arouses his compassion for what we are going through. In Jesus Christ there is mercy, as well as the power to give us victory. When struggles come we must take a deep breath and talk to God from the depth of our being, expressing exactly what we think and feel. As his children, the Lord knows what we are going through and how to meet our needs. But, as previously stated, it is essential that we exercise our faith by surrendering our will to God. Although we may not feel God's presence, we can stand firm on the promises found in his Word.

Before entering the ministry I had a conversation with a clergy friend. He shared his frustration with me concerning problems in his parish. He was very frustrated, telling me that he was unleashing his anger in his prayers. When he told me how he was expressing himself to God, I was surprised and even shocked. Although he did not use profanity, his prayers reflected stark language that resulted from his pain. While his approach to God was questionable to me at that time, I am certain that the Lord considered not only his anguish, but also his love for Jesus Christ and his commitment to the Church.

We are not promised a trouble free life, but those who walk in faith are promised sustaining grace. The apostle Paul alluded to his challenges when he compared the Christian life to a race that involves discipline, endurance, and pain. (I Corinthians 9:24-27) Paul warns us about being controlled by negativity, rather than learning from our past and moving forward with our lives. The valleys and shadows of life are not obstacles to retreat from, but rather motivators to move us into a prayerful relationship with God. In Jesus we have an intercessor who feels our pain and offers us a sanctuary, where we can regain our strength and direction. This speaks to those areas in life where victory has not yet been achieved. We come to the Lord as sinners, praying for the grace that will lead us to holiness.

Prayers of the Heart

For many years my prayers were primarily a structured and ritualistic exercise that lacked honesty, depth, and feeling. I grew up in a liturgical church where printed prayers were cited, and there was no teaching or encouragement to pray from the heart. In a sense, I was talking at God instead of offering myself up to him. After years of a sporadic and rather shallow approach to prayer, I realized that prayer is an honest sharing of who we are and where we are in life. It was then that I began to speak to the Lord about my temptations, needs, concerns, and fears. And yes, I even brought my frustrations and anger to God. This turning point began a journey that took me to new heights and a deeper relationship with my Creator.

Prayer has many facets, but at its center there is wholeheartedness, which is simply a pure and honest heart. Excellent examples of this are found in the Psalms, including David's prayer in Psalm 25:

> To you, O Lord, I lift up my soul; in you I trust, O my God. Do not let me be put to shame, nor let my enemies triumph over me. No one whose hope is in you will ever be put to shame. Remember not the

sins of my youth and my rebellious ways; according to your love remember me, for you are good, O Lord. For the sake of your name, O Lord, forgive my iniquity, though it is great. Turn to me and be gracious to me, for I am lonely and afflicted. The troubles of my heart have multiplied; free me from anguish. Look upon my affliction and my distress. (Psalm 25:1-3,6,7,16-18)

In this prayer David reached down into the depth of his soul and brought his burdens to the Lord, trusting God to bring him peace and to meet his needs. Rather than a mechanical communication, this is a prayer that radiates from David's heart, manifesting his true feelings and concerns. Without pride or reservation, he called to the Lord from his sorrow and pain. His supplications reveal an inner conflict and honesty that opened a channel for God's mercy.

An important element in Psalm 25 is David's patience in waiting upon the Lord. He wrote, "Guide me in your truth and teach me, for you are my God and Savior, and my hope is in you all day long." (Psalm 25:5) Other translations read, "In thee I wait all day long." David patiently waited upon God for guidance and solutions to his problems. His expectancy was rooted both in the Lord's promises and how God had previously responded to his prayers. Although patience is required in all areas of life, few people realize the importance of this gift in their spiritual life. In our technical and fast moving world, patience is seldom a discipline that is practiced or sought through prayer. But the lack of patience has erosive effects upon our spiritual life. This is a subject that we will examine more thoroughly in Chapter Three.

This psalm also reveals David imploring God to search his heart for existing sin, so that he might be cleansed and renewed through repentance. Prayers of this nature are often difficult, due to the pain that is associated with God's probing light. Divine convictions confront our denials and pride, both of which are barriers to a pure relationship with God. But these are the prayers that bring us closer to the Lord. How can we change unless we honestly look within ourselves and offer up areas of concern? The inability or refusal to be honest with God is a primary reason why people remain static in their spiritual journey.

We live in a world of deception, half-truths, and distortion, all of which have become infused into the psyche. Needless to say, this baggage has a destructive impact on all of our relationships. Like David, God wants us to come to him with a pure and honest heart, thereby allowing him to administer the transforming grace that brings renewal and leads us to holiness. David approached God in such a manner with these words:

> O Lord, you have searched me and you know me. You know when I sit down and when I rise; you perceive my thoughts from afar. You discern my going out and my lying down; you are familiar with all my ways. Before a word is on my tongue you know it completely, O Lord. Search me, O God and know my heart; test me and know my anxious thoughts. See if there is any offensive way in me, and lead me in the way everlasting. (Psalm 138:1-4, 23,24)

Solitude and Silence

The Sons of Korah wrote, "Be still, and know that I am God; I will be exalted among the nations, I will be exalted in the earth."

(Psalm 46:10) The ancients knew that times of solitude and silence better enabled them to hear God's voice. The Lord beckons us from societal distractions, in order that our spirits might become one with his. Jesus began his ministry in the desert, where he could quiet his emotions and be attentive to his inner life and the Father's will. In solitude and silence he prepared himself for his mission to a lost and dying world. Likewise, the prophet Elijah found strength in the wilderness, where he heard the soft voice of God, saying to him:

> Go out and stand on the mountain in the presence of the Lord, for the Lord is about to pass by. The great and powerful wind tore the mountains apart and shattered the rocks before the Lord, but the Lord was not in the wind. After the wind there was an earthquake, but the Lord was not in the earthquake. After the earthquake came a fire, but the Lord was not in the fire. After the fire came a gentle whisper. When Elijah heard it, he pulled his cloak over his face and went out and stood at the mouth of the cave. (I Kings 19:11-13)

Knowing God's awesome power as the Creator and sustainer of the universe, Elijah expected the Lord to be revealed in one of nature's mighty displays, but that was not the case. The Lord was not found in the wind, earthquake, or fire. Instead, Elijah learned that God speaks to the heart in places of solitude and silence. For some reason we have difficulty quieting our spirits and spending time alone with the Lord. Maybe our fast moving society and the belief that accomplishments come through activity, has something to do with it. But God calls us from life's noisy distractions and influences that our spirits might become one with his.

In his book *The Way of the Heart*, Henri J.M. Nouwen provides helpful insights into the lives of the desert fathers who resided in Egypt during the fourth and fifth centuries. These mystics sought to escape from the world's negative influences and forces. The words *flee, silence,* and *prayer,* summarized their spiritual philosophy and quest for a deeper meaning in life. (Nouwen 1981, pp. 3,4) In their striving to become sensitive to the Spirit's voice and become one with God, they chose to abandon worldly desires and burdens. Those who fled to the desert were not concerned with institutional religion, for they believed that the inner life could only be experienced and nurtured by withdrawing from life's distractions.

Although we have chosen to live a different lifestyle, it is important that we take time away from activities and hectic schedules to commune with God. It is during these quiet times that we become more aware of our inner life. This translates into realized needs that only God can satisfy. Stillness is not merely relaxation, but rather moving from the physical senses to a spiritual dimension where there is inner healing. Our desert experiences enable us to see the dark shadows of the soul, as well as the Lord's merciful presence. In this state we also touch the unconscious, bringing repressed matter to the surface for prayer and restoration.

It was in the desert where John the Baptist was prepared as the forerunner to Christ. In the desolation of the wilderness God prepared him to proclaim the message of repentance that would pave the way for Jesus. John's time alone with the Lord gave him the assurance of his call, equipping him to be a fearless preacher of truth. This uneducated man stood up against powerful individuals and the political system of his day, and it all began in the Judean wilderness where he heard the voice of God.

We are to follow the example of Jesus, who often left the

crowds to spend time alone with the Father. He went into the hills and to lonely places where he would sometimes spend all night praying. (Matthew 14:23; Mark 6:46; Luke 5:15; 6:12) On one occasion, Jesus took Peter, John, and James, to a high mountain where the three apostles observed him praying. It was on this mountain that Jesus was transformed and where Elijah and Moses appeared. (Luke 9:28-36) A favorite place for Jesus to pray was the Garden of Gethsemane on the Mount of Olives. This was just beyond the Kidron Valley near the city of Jerusalem. Gethsemane was a quiet place of retreat and rest for our Savior and his disciples. (Luke 22:39-45) It was in such places that Jesus encouraged his disciples to pray. (Matthew 6:5,6)

Instead of retreating to places of solitude and silence, we often pray on the run. Few people take time out of their day to silently journey within and allow the Spirit to speak to them. This is also true of the clergy, who maintain busy schedules. Needless to say, if pastors spent more quiet time with God they would have increased strength and discernment. In his book *The Eternal Now*, Paul Tillich wrote, "It is in the poverty of silence that God's riches come into view. May we dare to walk in solitude and silence—to face the Eternal, to find others, to clearly see ourselves." (Tillich 1963, pp. 25,34)

Praying in Faith

Beginning with the Book of Genesis and through the last chapter of Revelation, the Bible underscores the need for faith. The Lord made it clear to the first man and woman that they were to trust him for everything. Unfortunately, we know the rest of the story. But the patriarchs were commended for their faith, including Jonah and Job, even though they had their issues and struggles. (Jonah 2:2; Job 13:15) It is Abraham, however, who will forever be known as the father of faith. Regarding Abraham's faith, Paul said:

> What then shall we say that Abraham, our forefather, discovered in the matter? If, in fact, Abraham was justified by works, he had something to boast about—but not before God. What does the Scripture say? Abraham believed God, and it was credited to him as righteousness. (Romans 4:1-3)

The faith of Moses provided the strength and endurance to lead the Israelites on a journey that took forty years. We cannot begin to comprehend the adversities that were endured in the desert. But Moses kept his faith in God, even when the people lost their trust in his leadership and the Lord's wisdom. The trials in the wilderness were relentless, but this servant of the Lord was obedient to the very end. Although he had times of anger and some doubt, in faith he accomplished his long and arduous mission.

It was their trust in God that empowered the prophets to utter divine truths at their own peril. Over the centuries they made repeated calls to the people, in which they echoed God's messages. These communications often addressed idol worship and the need for repentance, as well as issues relating to faith. To sternly declare God's Word, often in terms of his judgment upon an unrepentant nation, required a level of faith that is foreign to us. In their effort to be obedient to God, these men risked everything.

The psalms are filled with prayers expressing total trust in the Lord. King David, whose life began to erode because of personal sin and relational problems, often came to God with his trials. It was not unusual for David to convey his anger to the Lord, sometimes questioning God's presence. But David always rebounded with words of faith and praise. In one of his psalms he said, "The Lord is a refuge for the oppressed, a stronghold in times of trouble. Those who know your name will trust in you, for you, Lord, have never forsaken those who seek you." (Psalm 9:9,10) Again he wrote, "In you our fathers put their trust; they trusted, and you delivered them. They cried to you and were saved; in you they trusted and were not disappointed." (Psalm 22:4,5) David placed his hope in the Lord, knowing that his prayers would be answered. (Psalm 36:15) He exhorted the people to pour out their hearts to God and to expect God's mercy and grace. (Psalm 17:6; 62:8)

King Solomon, known for his wisdom, was a leader whose life manifested a deep faith in God. In the Book of Proverbs he provides insights into many facets of life, including one's relationship with God. In his writings, intended for all Israel, he wrote, "Trust in the Lord with all your heart and lean not on your own understanding; in all your ways acknowledge him, and he will make your paths straight." (Proverbs 3:5,6) Solomon saw God's Word as being flawless and his presence a shield for those of faith. (Proverbs 30:5) In Ecclesiastes he stressed that prayer is not simply talking to God, but it is also listening. (Ecclesiastes 5:1-3) This is an important reminder, for we tend to be quick to talk but have difficulty with silent listening.

Paul reminds us that faith is the essence of Christian living, a truth that speaks to our communications with the Lord. He told the Ephesians that they were saved by grace, which is made possible through faith. He also informed them that faith is not a result of works, but rather the fruit of the Spirit. (Ephesians 2:8,9; Galatians 5:22,23; Romans 1:17) According to Paul, faith is crucial to our prayer life and God's flow of grace into our lives.

Without faith, our prayers are merely verbal exercises that lack expectation.

Jesus told his disciples that faith is the leaven and channel through which divine gifts flow. He said, "If you believe, you will receive whatever you ask for in prayer." (Matthew 21:22) Mark records Jesus saying, "Whatever you ask for in prayer, believe that you have received it, and it will be yours." (Mark 11:24) This passage is often misunderstood, for it seems to indicate that God will satisfy all of our desires if we just have faith. The translation, however, must be seen within the context of God's will and the gifts of the Holy Spirit, which are offered to everyone who seeks them.

The author of Hebrews tells us to approach God's throne in confidence, with the full assurance of faith, both in God's existence, and that he will answer our prayers. (Hebrews 4:16; 10:22,23; 11:6) In his epistle to Christian Jews, the apostle James told the people that those who come to God in doubt are like waves of the sea that are blown and tossed about by the wind. He said that their doubt prevents them from receiving the Lord's gifts. (James 1:5-8) God will certainly respond, when in faith, we pray for the gifts that transform us and enable us to touch the lives of others.

Jesus is concerned about the whole person, but it grieved him when people only thought about physical and worldly matters. On one occasion he said, "Do not work for the food that spoils, but for the food that endures to eternal life, which the Son of Man will give you. On him the Father has placed his approval." (John 6:26,27) Our Savior was continuously confronted with individuals who were seeking physical cures, but very few came to him with matters of the soul. The people wanted Jesus to be both a political figure and a miracle worker, and when he did not respond, many people walked away from him. He once asked his disciples if they also were going to leave him, but Peter said, "Lord, to whom shall we go? You alone have the words of eternal life. We believe and know that you are the Holy One of God." (John 6:66-69)

When Jesus spoke about faith being the key to answered prayer, he was alluding to the spiritual gifts that glorify God. These are the gifts that Paul wrote about, which include: love, joy, peace, patience, kindness, goodness, faithfulness, gentleness, and self-control. (Galatians 5:22) While the Lord is concerned about all of our needs and will give us his sustaining grace, those who pray in faith for the gifts of the Spirit are assured of receiving them. God will never deny his life changing gifts to those who come in faith with a pure heart.

Prayers for Healing and Miracles

A controversy in some Christian communities is the subject of faith healing. Simply stated, does praying in faith result in bodily healing? Do New Testament teachings indicate this, or is this a false understanding of the scriptural passages, particularly those relating to the teachings and ministry of Jesus and his apostles? We are provided with instances in which Jesus clearly tells individuals that their faith has healed them. For example, Matthew records two healings that seem to support this truth. In one situation, Jesus healed a woman who suffered some manner of bleeding for a period of twelve years. When she reached out to Jesus, touching his robe, Jesus said to her, "Take heart, daughter, your faith has healed you." (Matthew 9:20-22) In another incident we learn of two blind men who followed Jesus, calling out to him for mercy. Jesus asked them if they believed that he had the power to cure them, and they responded that they did. He then touched their eyes, stating that they were healed as a result of their faith. (Matthew 9:27-31)

According to Mark, while in Jericho with his disciples, Jesus healed a blind man named Bartimaeus, who was beseeching the Lord for a cure. While the crowd tried to silence the man, Jesus responded with compassion, asking him what he wanted. The man said that he wanted to have sight, and the Lord told him to go, that his faith had healed him. (Mark 10:46-52) Luke also wrote of a healing that Jesus attributed to faith. While on his way to Jerusalem, Jesus was confronted by ten men who had leprosy. They cried out, knowing that he had miraculous power. Our Savior healed all ten, but only one thanked Jesus and praised God for the healing. After questioning the ingratitude of the other nine, our Lord informed the thankful man that his faith had made him well. (Luke 17:11-19) These are only a few examples of healings in which faith was a factor.

In the encounters mentioned, Jesus specifically stated that it was the person's faith that made the difference. In every case there was a manifestation of belief on the part of the recipients prior to their healing. If faith in Jesus Christ is the means through which we are physically healed, then one can assume that the Lord will intercede on behalf of all believers. If this is our premise based upon certain passages of scripture, why are individuals of deep faith and commitment not healed?

We must conclude that regardless how much faith we possess, there is no healing in this life apart from God's will. As such, our prayers may not bring the results we desire. During my ministries many people of faith have died from illnesses and accidents. Some of these individuals were children, which is extremely difficult for everyone. In one of my parishes I had two children who died when a tornado struck our small community. The obvious question is why God allowed this to occur. These youth were involved in church life, and they had the faith that the Lord speaks about.

Except for the intercessory healings performed by Jesus, and the power that he gave his disciples to perform such miracles, the Scriptures do not promise us healing based upon our faith. In fact, beginning with the apostles, countless people have suffered and died because of their faith. According to tradition, eleven of the twelve apostles were martyred for preaching the gospel and proclaiming Jesus as the Messiah. The apostle Paul is a prime example of persecution, suffering, and martyrdom. After Paul's conversion, God told the disciple Ananias that Paul would suffer greatly for the gospel. (Acts 9:13-16) This became a reality, for he experienced more recorded hardships than any other follower of Christ. Paul was continuously harassed and the victim of violence. He even reported living with chronic pain, which he referred to as a thorn in the flesh. Although we can only speculate what caused his suffering, we do know that he prayed for relief. He wrote to the Corinthians that he pleaded with the Lord to remove the pain, but instead of healing Paul, God told him to lean upon divine grace. (II Corinthians 12:7-10) Paul eventually was imprisoned in Rome, where he was executed under the rule of Nero.

Both the Scriptures and the history of the Church reveal that great people of faith have suffered and met death through both martyrdom and disease. Christians are not promised a life void of suffering, nor are they promised healing through prayers of faith. However, as in Paul's situation, we are promised God's empowering and sustaining grace. This is not to say that it is wrong to pray for physical cures, but we must remember that our lives are in the care and will of God. Whether in life or death, we belong to the Lord. We should also note that death is the ultimate healer of our earthly infirmities. This, of course, is also a matter of faith. Actually, both disease and imminent death put our faith to the test. Pastors spend many hours with dying individuals, and they know how faith brings peace and assurance. It is faith that prepares a person to leave this life.

Recently, a pastor friend of mine died after serving the Lord for thirty-three years. Upon retirement, he learned that he had terminal cancer. It was difficult to see him suffer with this terrible disease. He spent his life with others in similar situations, always being there for them and their families. As he struggled, trying to maintain a glimmer of hope for a miracle, I found myself pondering the injustices of this life. I thought about the many people of faith who had prayed for his recovery, which did not occur. My thoughts then drifted to the suffering and death of Jesus and the promise found in his words and resurrection. During this time I realized how focused we are upon this life and the physical world. Even though we speak about eternity and the glory of God's kingdom, it is difficult to let go of what we can presently see and touch.

A situation etched in my memory were the seven hours I spent with a death row inmate prior to his execution. The state prison where I served as the Protestant chaplain was the location for Pennsylvania's first execution in thirty-three years. The prisoner, who was a Christian, shared his life with me, including the circumstances that led to his crime. We prayed together, received the Eucharist, and engaged in personal conversation until the time of his execution. As he approached his death there was a peaceful presence that could not be denied. There was also a deep sadness on the part of the prison staff. In the midst of these emotions was a prisoner whose faith in Jesus Christ was evident. No one at the execution could dispute that he was at peace and filled with the love of Christ.

Although many people were praying for a miracle, which in this case meant a stay of execution, it did not happen. There was even a last minute telephone call from a government official, but in a matter of minutes the young man was put to death. It was difficult to believe that I was witnessing the execution of someone that I had just spent seven hours with and came to know as a forgiven sinner and Christian. This, however, was the stark reality.

When executions are scheduled, groups opposed to the death penalty gather to make their beliefs and feelings known. Some of these groups maintain an organized structure and become involved with media interviews and vigils at the execution sites. Among these persons are Christians and religious leaders who engage in intercessory prayer. The activities take place at churches, as well as outside the prisons. It is difficult to say how influential the gatherings are, or whether their prayers have any impact upon the death penalty. It is true, however, that even with their intercessory prayer, death row inmates continue to be executed. Regardless of the inmate's faith and the prayers of thousands of individuals, the sentences are carried out, unless a legal matter develops.

The New Testament records thirty-five healings performed by Jesus, which include three instances when he raised individuals from the dead. While these were acts of compassion, Jesus used them to glorify God and to lay the foundation for his ministry. His healings authenticated his divinity, thereby validating his teachings and prophecies. They were also a graphic and convincing announcement that his presence brought the kingdom of God to the people. When Jesus told certain individuals that their faith healed them, he was emphasizing the necessity to trust him for all things, particularly for their forgiveness and salvation. Those who witnessed these miraculous events would also be drawn to the person of Jesus, as we are today when we read the New Testament accounts.

Although God does heal people today, the incidents recorded in the Scriptures are not a promise that he will heal us. To assume this is a misunderstanding of the passages and their context. Actually, it is when we are not cured that our faith is tested. Furthermore, faith healing has proven to be a dangerous assumption, resulting in the death of some people who were convinced that they no longer needed life sustaining medications. Also, it is not unusual for Christians to be consumed by guilt when they are not healed, believing that their faith was not strong enough, Those who seek healing should combine their prayers with medical treatment. Sometimes we forget that the medical profession is a gift that God has given to everyone.

The misuse of God's Word can be very destructive, especially when it comes to health issues. There is a difference between trusting in God's sustaining grace and putting him to the test for something he has not promised. Needless to say, even if the Lord intercedes and heals us of a particular illness, we will eventually be overtaken by a medical condition that will result in our death. This should not cast a shadow over us, but rather align our expectations in accordance with God's promises. While we should pray for miracles, we must realize that healing lies within God's will, and accepting his will speaks to our faith.

The Lord called Job a righteous man, but this did not prevent Job's suffering. Even when Job's life was restored, the scars of his pain and loss remained. In Gethsemane we see the pain that sometimes accompanies God's will. Jesus prayed to the Father, asking that the cup of suffering might pass him by. But our Savior knew that his suffering and death would transform the lives of people, bringing hope to a lost world. The prophet Isaiah wrote, "After the suffering of his soul, he will see the light of life and be satisfied; by his knowledge my righteous servant will justify many, and he will bear their iniquities. For he bore the sins of many and made intercession for the transgressors." (Isaiah 53:12) Jesus willingly submitted to the Father's will in order to bring salvation to the world. Although our knowledge and understanding is limited, there is no doubt that some of our trials also serve a higher purpose.

Like our Savior, Paul understood his struggles as a way to bring glory to God. His faith and commitment did not remove him from struggle and pain. Actually, many of his trials were related to his faith and ministry. But Paul leaned upon the Lord for sustaining grace, knowing that in his weakness lay the power of God. Both Paul's writings and those of Luke tell us volumes about trusting in God when physical pain is not removed through prayer. Rather than Paul's faith removing him from adversity, it was his physical pain that drew him closer to God. His trials became the source for increased faith, inner strength, and hope.

Our faith must rely upon God's perfect wisdom, which means trusting him when our prayers seem to go unanswered. While we should never abandon our prayers for bodily healing, there must be a willingness to accept the Lord's will in all circumstances. Whether the situation pertains to us or someone else, we are to trust in God's presence and mercy.

Reasoning with God

The Bible reports situations in which individuals are found reasoning with the Lord. For example, Moses asked God not to judge Israel when they fashioned an idol in the form of a calf. This wilderness incident manifested the rebellion of the people, who lost faith in both God and Moses. The Lord told Moses that he was going to destroy the Israelites for their disobedience and idolatry. But anticipating how the Egyptians would respond if God carried out his judgment, Moses reasoned with the Lord, saying:

> Why should your anger burn against your people, who you brought out of Egypt with great power and a mighty hand? Why should the Egyptians say, 'It was with evil intent that he brought them out, to kill them in the mountains and to wipe them off the face of the earth'? Turn from your fierce anger; relent and do not bring disaster on your people. Remember your servants, Abraham, Isaac and Jacob, to whom you swore by your own self; 'I will make your descendants as numerous as the stars in the sky, and I will give your descendants all this land I promised them, and it will be their inheritance forever.' Then the Lord relented and did not bring on his people the disaster he had threatened. (Exodus 32:11-14; cp. Numbers 14:13-23)

These are strong words from a servant of God, and I am certain that some readers find them discomforting, or doubt that Moses ever spoke to the Lord in this manner. Was Moses trying to manipulate God or scold him for his anger and talk of judgment? When examining the circumstances one must conclude that neither is the case. The Lord placed Moses in a position of leadership over the Jews, and this brought a sense of responsibility for their welfare and salvation. As such, Moses was simply responding to his burden for a people who were struggling with a life that took them from bondage to the harsh realities of the wilderness. He was also concerned how the Egyptians would interpret a divine judgment on the people. Moses had given up his life for this mission from God, and he felt the need to express himself.

Like a defense attorney preparing a court case for a client, Moses presented God with reasons why the people should survive. He even told the Lord that if the people were not forgiven, then he no longer wished to live. In this statement he was pouring out his soul in bewilderment and emotional pain. This visceral announcement influenced God to spare the people. The Lord did, however, tell Moses that the Israelites would eventually be punished for their sin, which we learn was a plague brought upon Aaron and the people. God said to Moses:

> Whoever has sinned against me I will blot out of my book. Now go, lead the people to the place I spoke of, and my angel will go before you. However, when the time comes for me to punish, I will punish them for their sin. And the Lord struck the people with a plague because of what they did with the calf Aaron had made. (Exodus 32:33-35)

Other individuals who reasoned with God include Gideon, who asked the Lord to communicate with him in a very unusual manner. Gideon said to the Lord, "If you will save Israel by my hand as you have promised, I will place a wool fleece on the threshing floor. If there is dew only on the fleece and all the ground is dry, then I will know that you will save Israel by my hand." (Judges 6:36,37) After God responded to this first request, Gideon asked the Lord for a second proof, and it also was granted. He said to the Lord, "Do not be angry with me. Let me make just one more request. Allow me one more test with the fleece. This time make the fleece dry and the ground covered with dew. That night God did so. Only the fleece was dry; all the ground was covered with dew." (verses 39,40)

The Scriptures also reveal that Hannah, the barren wife of a Levite named Elkanah, reasoned with God to give her a son. She promised God that if she were gifted with a son, she would dedicate him to the Lord's service. With deep emotion she prayed, "O Lord Almighty, if you will only look upon your servant's misery and remember me, and not forget your servant, but give her a son, then I will give him to the Lord for all the days of his life, and no razor will ever be used on his head." (I Samuel 1:11) In the course of time, Hannah conceived and gave birth to a son. She named him Samuel, which means *asked of God.* (I Samuel 1:20) Hannah kept her promise, dedicating her son as a Nazarite. As soon as he was weaned she brought him to Shiloh, where she presented him to Eli the priest, to begin his service to the Lord.

We cannot know the wisdom of God in these situations, but we are assured that he hears the concerns of his faithful children. In each of these instances God responded to the reasoning and will of individuals, but it seems that the requests fit into his sovereignty and providence. The Lord's decisions reflect not only his compassion, but also his perfect and infinite knowledge. We can be certain that God responds to human reasoning when it speaks to our spiritual growth, service to others, and the building of his kingdom.

Repentance and Humility

We are to approach the Lord in humility and with an attitude of repentance, recognizing that we are sinners in need of continuing grace. The inner cleansing that comes through repentance reconciles us with God and fills us with his peace. When the prophet Isaiah was commissioned by the Lord, he considered himself an unclean sinner. In his reaction to God's call, he shouted, "Woe is me! I am ruined! For I am a man of unclean lips, and my eyes have seen the King, the Lord Almighty." (Isaiah 6:5) Upon saying this, one of the seraphs of the Lord flew to him with a live coal in his hand, which he had taken with tongs from the altar. He touched Isaiah's mouth with the hot coal and said, "See, this has touched your lips; your guilt is taken away and your sin is atoned for." (Isaiah 6:6,7)

It was Isaiah's humility, repentant heart, and confession that brought him into God's fellowship and service. This is the means through which we receive forgiveness and begin our spiritual journey. The heart of God is stirred when we acknowledge that we are unclean and in need of grace. Just the thought of the Lord knowing our sinful desires should bring us to our knees, but unfortunately the lack of sensitivity to the Spirit's convictions makes people insensitive to their present and eternal needs. The writer of Hebrews emphasized this when he said, "Encourage one another daily, as long as it is called Today, so that none of you may be hardened by sin's deceitfulness." (Hebrews 3:13) Like Jesus' lesson on the four soils, the seed that falls on the hard path does not penetrate the soil. Although the seed is good, the hardness of the soil rejects it. This is a graphic picture of the heart that has become callous to God's truth and mercy. It is a tragedy to see human pride lead people down the path of destruction. King David knew both the pain of guilt and the need for forgiveness. These are his words:

> Blessed is he whose transgressions are forgiven, whose sins are covered. Blessed is the man whose sin the Lord does not count against him and in whose

spirit is no deceit. When I kept silent, my bones wasted away through my groaning all day long. For day and night your hand was heavy upon me; my strength was sapped as in the heat of summer. Then I acknowledged my sin to you and did not cover up my iniquity. I said, 'I will confess my transgressions to the Lord'—and you forgave the guilt of my sin. Therefore, let everyone who is godly pray to you while you may be found. (Psalm 32:1-6)

David reached a point when he could no longer bear the burden of his guilt. In this particular confession, which may be related to his sins with Bathsheba, he pours out his soul to the Lord. He also alludes to the blessings that accompany repentance and confession, and he encourages others to bring their sins to God. (verses 6-10) David's prayer of confession speaks to everyone, for we have all experienced the weight of sin, and we know the cleansing that takes place through confession. A repentant heart continuously looks within for areas of unrighteousness that need to be brought before God's throne of grace.

During my prison ministry I discovered that most inmates carry intense guilt resulting from their crimes and lifestyle. Even though some prisoners do not openly admit to feelings of remorse because of the machismo factor, denial, or continuing legal pursuits, most of them experience shame for their sins. Without repentance, their inner conflict hinders the opportunity for a new life. The negativity and stress of prison adds additional obstacles to spiritual development. But people in society also find themselves confronted with similar situations. Regardless where we are in life, there is always the need for self-examination and repentance.

An essential ingredient of repentance is humility, which is a virtue that Jesus often emphasized in his teachings. He addressed this subject with his apostles, whose remarks and actions sometimes manifested sinful pride. The parable of the *Pharisee and the Tax Collector* is an excellent example of our Savior's lessons on both repentance and humility. In this story, Jesus said:

> Two men went up to the temple to pray, one a Pharisee and the other a tax collector. The Pharisee stood up and prayed about himself; 'God, I thank you that I am not like other men—robbers, evil doers, adulterers—or even like this tax collector. I fast twice a week and give a tenth of all I get.' But the tax collector stood at a distance. He would not even look up to heaven, but beat his breast and said, 'God, have mercy on me, a sinner.' I tell you that this man, rather than the other, went home justified before God. For everyone who exalts himself will be humbled, and he who humbles himself will be exalted. (Luke 18:9-14)

The Pharisee in this story was filled with pride and self-righteousness. Instead of seeing himself as a sinner in need of forgiving grace, he compared himself with others and boasted before the Lord. He even belittled the tax collector, whom he believed to be a real sinner. Unfortunately, the world is full of people, who like the Pharisee, fail to see themselves as sinners. But the prophet Isaiah said, "How can we be saved? All of us have become like one who is unclean, and all our righteous acts are like filthy rags; we all shrivel up like a leaf, and like the wind our sins sweep us away." (Isaiah 64:5,6) Paul wrote, "all have sinned and fall short of the glory of God, and are justified freely by his grace through the redemption that came through Christ Jesus." (Romans 3:23,24) The apostle James emphasizes the importance of works, meaning that out lives are to reflect our discipleship. While this is true, it does not suggest that we become righteous through works alone. It is our faith in Jesus Christ that makes us righteous before God, but faith cannot exist without a humble and contrite heart that leads to serving God and one another.

The Lord does not want us to live in defeat, wallowing in a past that has been forgiven. We are called to rejoice in our forgiveness and to celebrate spiritual victories, as we move toward increased understanding and holiness. It is important, however, that we never forget where we came from and the continuing reality of sinful influences. Humility and repentance are the virtues that keep us strong in our faith. Although the Christian life is a sanctifying process in which we increase in love for God and one another, it is not a life that is void of trial and sin.

The Lord said to King Solomon, "If my people, who are called by my name, will humble themselves and pray and seek my face and turn from their wicked ways, then I will hear from heaven and will forgive their sin and will heal their land." (II Chronicles 7:14) This message applies to the Church, for humility is the essence of our Savior's ministry and the means through which we approach God. But are we a humble people? Do we pray for this gift that unites us with the Lord and brings about relational harmony? Our model for humility is Jesus, who emptied himself of divine glory to become a servant and sacrificial offering for humanity.

Matthew records a conversation that the apostles had with Jesus. They wanted to know which of them would be the greatest in his kingdom. They believed that their sacrifices were deserving of rewards, especially since they left everything to follow him. To their surprise, Jesus informed them that they were misunderstanding the kingdom of God, and he took advantage of their question to teach them an important truth. Jesus summoned a little child to his side and said, "I tell you the truth, unless you change and become like little children, you will never see the kingdom of heaven. Therefore, whoever humbles himself like this child is the greatest in the kingdom of heaven." (Matthew 18:3,4)

In this brief response, Jesus was telling his apostles to live a life of humility. Like their Savior, they were to see humanity through his eyes, recognizing that greatness is found in being a servant to all people. This revelation probably came as a shock to some of the apostles, who were undoubtedly beginning to believe that they were special. But practicing humility continues to be a radical teaching, for seldom do people think in these terms. After all, how can one who serves another be great? Society teaches that greatness is found in wealth, position, and power. It is a person's achievements that make them great, not bending down assuming the role of a servant. The lack of humility has always been a stumbling block, even for professing Christians.

Humility is not a gift that we are born with, but rather one that comes through desire and continuous prayer. Recognizing this truth, the apostle Paul exhorted the churches to strive for the spirit of a servant. He wrote the Philippian church, saying:

> Your attitude should be the same as that of Christ Jesus, who, being in the very nature of God, did not consider equality with God something to be grasped, but made himself nothing, taking the very nature of a servant, being made in human likeness. And being found in appearance as a man, he humbled himself and became obedient to death—even death on a cross! Therefore God exalted him to the highest place and gave him the name that is above every

name, that at the name of Jesus every knee should bow, in heaven and on earth and under the earth, and every tongue confess that Jesus Christ is Lord, to the glory of God the Father. (Philippians 2:5-11)

Paul encouraged followers to live the golden rule by being humble, considering others as being better than themselves, thereby bringing glory to Christ. John the Baptist told the people that he had to decrease, in order that all glory be given to Jesus. He said, "The one who comes from above is above all; the one who is from the earth belongs to the earth, and speaks as one from the earth. The one who comes from heaven is above all. He testifies to what he has seen and heard." (John 3:31,32) The recognition of who we are, and of our total dependence upon God, is the first step toward humility.

Righteous Relationships

Jesus teaches that we are to make every effort to be at peace with others, including those whom we perceive to be our enemies. Our Savior clearly states that God only hears the prayers of those with a pure heart, and this speaks to our relationships. Jesus said, "When you stand praying, if you hold anything against anyone, forgive them, so that your Father in heaven may forgive your sins." (Mark 11:25; cp. Matthew 6:14,15) The Lord knows if we are harboring sinful thoughts or emotions toward another person. God also knows if we have taken the necessary steps to forgive and reconcile with others.

In his book, *The Cost of Discipleship*, Dietrich Bonhoeffer stresses that God's grace is not cheap, meaning that our salvation has come at a high cost. (Bonhoeffer, 1949, 45-60) Who can begin to comprehend the physical, emotional, and spiritual pain that Jesus endured for all sinners? Yet, we are often unwilling to work at improving our relationships. Rather than being peace makers as Jesus commands, some people intentionally nurture their grievances and anger. The love for others is woven into our love for God, for we cannot truly love the Lord if we fail to love one another. To harbor animosity toward another person is to violate God's two greatest commandments. While it is difficult to maintain good relationships with everyone, we are called to pray about situations that concern us. This means praying for the other person, as well as our own feelings. In following the teachings of Jesus, Paul shared these words with the Christians in Rome:

> Do not repay anyone evil for evil. Be careful to do what is right in the eyes of everybody. If it is possible, as far as it depends on you, live at peace with everyone. Do not take revenge my friends, but leave room for God's wrath, for it is written: 'It is mine to avenge; I will repay,' says the Lord. On the contrary: 'If your enemy is hungry, feed him; if he is thirsty, give him something to drink. In doing this, you will heap burning coals on his head.' Do not be overcome by evil, but overcome evil with good. (Romans 12:17-21)

The teachings of Jesus go far beyond simply being at peace with one another. Matthew records the following words of Jesus:

> You have heard it said, 'Love your neighbor and hate your enemy.' But I tell you: Love your enemies and pray for those who persecute you, that you may be sons of your Father in heaven. He causes his sun to

rise on the evil and the good, and sends rain on the righteous and unrighteous. If you love those who love you, what reward will you get? Are not even the tax collectors doing that? And if you greet only your brothers, what are you doing more than others? Do not even pagans do that? Be perfect, therefore, as your heavenly Father is perfect. (Matthew 5:43-48)

Shortly after Jesus chose his twelve apostles, he began to teach them about the kingdom of God. On one occasion he said:

If someone strikes you on one cheek, turn to him the other also. If someone takes your cloak, do not stop him from taking your tunic. Give to everyone who asks you, and if anyone takes what belongs to you, do not demand it back. Do to others, as you would have them do to you. (Luke 6:29-31)

These words seem extreme, for they suggest that Christians should allow themselves to be taken advantage of by other people. Is this the interpretation that Jesus intended, or should we understand it in another way? One cannot imagine our Savior asking us to be abused by others for the purpose of love. After all, a significant aspect of love involves accountability and justice. Therefore, to literally interpret these passages is to miss the intended message. Jesus was trying to implant a certain attitude and way of life for his disciples, one that centered upon compassion, giving, and self-sacrifice. The wording in this lesson is intended to emphasize the need for a pure heart. Although his apostles would struggle with this teaching, they certainly remembered the point of the lesson. Their path was to be one of understanding and peace, which at times would necessitate personal sacrifice.

Prison inmates often engage in manipulative practices, both with their peers and staff. This occurs even when there is no devious motive. Prison life is one of physical and emotional survival, and it is natural for inmates to find ways to deal with their stressful environment. Having been a pastor to a large prison population, there was always a concern about being manipulated. As such, I had to carefully examine my relationships within the context of each situation. This was particularly true with prisoners who worked for me in the chapel. However, when I became too stringent in my relationships, it affected my ability to share the love of Christ. These are difficult ministries, and one must continuously seek a balance without compromising security standards. I made every effort to allow the flexibility that enabled inmates to experience the compassion of Jesus within necessary boundaries.

As Jesus reveals, sometimes we must allow this same flexibility in our relationships. Rather than laying down strict guidelines and ultimatums, self-sacrifice for the sake of love is needed. This does not mean that we accept abuse in order to be a Christian, but we should strive to be understanding and tolerant of another person's faults. This means lowering our expectations and loving all people, because Jesus has called us to be compassionate. The ministry of Christ reveals that he touched the lives of everyone with whom he interacted, meeting them where they were in life. Although our Lord hates sin, he loves the person, which is a distinction that we must make.

Paul told the Galatians that they were to love all people, with special attention given to their relationships with believers. This seems to imply that we are to love Christians more than others, but this is not what Paul is saying. He knew that the church in

Galatia was experiencing conflict and divisions over both secular and spiritual matters, and he was emphasizing the need for tolerance and love within the body of Christ. When, in the midst of our differences, we are united in love, we become witnesses who communicate the teachings of Jesus Christ. (Galatians 6:10) There will always be different opinions amongst people, but diversity enables objectivity and personal growth.

A person's anger brings an inner conflict that robs them of God's peace. During a teaching session with his disciples Jesus spoke about anger, saying, "You have heard that it was said to people long ago, do not murder, and anyone who murders will be subject to judgment. But I tell you that anyone who is angry with his brother will be subject to judgment." (Matthew 5:21,22) These strong words are seldom heard from church pulpits, but the need for righteous relationships cannot be separated from the gospel message and our Savior's lessons on prayer. At the center of life are relationships, and we are called to be peacemakers. (Matthew 5:9)

Before Jesus was arrested he promised his disciples an inner peace that is not of this world. (John 14:27) This promise echoes Paul's words to the Colossians when he wrote, "Let the peace of Christ rule in your hearts, since as members of one body you were called to peace." (Colossians 3:15) Although this peace does not remove us from life's trials, including relational difficulties, it does enable compassion, understanding, and tolerance toward others. This is the peace that is experienced when interacting with Spirit filled individuals, and it has the power to eliminate anger, bringing calm to troubled relationships.

Instead of being ruled by God's inner peace, people often allow negative emotions to control them. Christians may be united in Christ, but sin sometimes blocks the movement of the Holy Spirit acting upon the heart and tongue. In his epistle to

Christian Jews, the apostle James emphasized the perils of the tongue with these words:

> When we put bits into the mouths of horses to make them obey us, we can turn the whole animal. Or take ships as an example. Although they are so large and are driven by strong winds, they are steered by a very small rudder wherever the pilot wants to go. Likewise the tongue is a small part of the body, but it makes great boasts. Consider what a great forest is set on fire by a small spark. The tongue also is a fire, a world of evil among the parts of the body. It corrupts the whole person, sets the whole course of his life on fire, and is itself set on fire by hell. (James 3:3-6)

James continued this passage by telling his readers that the tongue can both praise God and curse others, but in reality there is only one voice that emanates from us, for fresh water and salt water cannot flow from the same spring. (verses 7-12) Words can wound us in ways that are difficult to recover from and erase. The emotional results of verbal abuse sometimes remain with a person for many years. The direction of one's life may even be influenced by what someone said to them years earlier. What we say to others, including the tone we use, is a reflection of our inner life. Replacing sin with love begins and continues with prayer. Developing a servant's attitude toward others requires honesty before God, with the continuous seeking of inner transformation. Paul refers to this spiritual quickening as the circumcision of the heart. In Judaism the outer sign or symbol of spiritual life for the male was physical circumcision, but Paul told the people that the real circumcision is the changed heart.

Being merciful toward one another is a theme that runs through the Bible, and it is at the core of Jesus' life and teachings. The heart of God is one of compassion and mercy, without which we would continue to walk in a hopeless state of darkness. In his *Sermon on the Mount*, also known as the *Beatitudes*, Jesus told his disciples that God's mercy is given to those who show mercy. (Matthew 5:7) To the religious leaders, he said, "Woe to you, teachers of the law and Pharisees, you hypocrites! You give a tenth of your spices, but you have neglected the most important matters of the law—justice, mercy and faithfulness." (Matthew 23:23) We are to prayerfully strive for the mercy that is found in Jesus Christ, and to share his mercy in our relationships.

The disciples often spoke about our Savior's command to be merciful to one another. The apostle James used uncompromising words when he wrote, "Judgment without mercy will be shown to anyone who has not been merciful. Mercy triumphs over judgment." (James 2:13) This inspired statement reveals how important it is to nurture our relationships through prayer and acts of kindness. God's intention is that we set aside all malice, and become the one humanity that we were created to be.

Regardless how strained a relationship becomes, we must do everything possible to bring about reconciliation. Rather than waiting for the other person to respond, the Scriptures teach that we are to take the initiative to establish peace. Jesus told his disciples that peacemakers receive God's blessings. Whether it is on a personal basis between two individuals or on an international level, relational harmony is God's command. We tend to make excuses, stating that relational peace is not possible. But this conclusion is often derived without prayer and concrete initiatives. Sometimes we forget that God is the initiator of our reconciliation with him. Jesus came for those lost in sin, and he died for the ungodly. In following our Savior's example, we are called to take the initiative to seek reconciliation with all people.

Persistent and Fervent Prayer

Jesus' parable of the *Persistent Widow* is a lesson on the importance of unceasing prayer. The Lord knows our needs before we come to him in prayer, but it is our sustained communion with him that reflects our true needs, desires, and burdens of the heart. To accentuate the necessity for fervent prayer, Jesus told this parable:

> In a certain town there was a judge who neither feared God nor cared about men. And there was a widow in that town who kept coming to him with the plea, 'Grant me justice against my adversary.' For some time he refused. But finally he said to himself, 'Even though I don't fear God or care about men, I will see that she gets justice, so that she won't eventually wear me out with her coming!' And the Lord said, listen to what the unjust judge says. And will not God bring about justice for his chosen ones who cry to him day and night? Will he keep putting them off? I tell you, he will see that they get justice, and quickly. However, when the Son of Man comes, will he find faith on the earth? (Luke 18:1-8)

Although this passage speaks about prayer within the context of justice, it teaches the importance of being persistent with situations that concern us. In this case, it was a matter of obtaining justice from an obstinate and uncaring judge. The widow reveals a deep sense of hopelessness, for she had no one to represent her as an intercessor. In the end it was only her persistence that led to satisfactory results. The judge finally responded to her simply because she was an annoyance. The judge did not care about the woman or the concept of justice. Instead, he only wanted to rid himself of an aggravation.

In this story Jesus points out that if an unjust judge responds to persistence, how much more will God respond to his children who cry out to him with their pleas. Matters that concern us will not go unanswered, for the Lord cares about our burdens and trials. In fact, it is our persistence that tells God just how concerned we are, and in his perfect knowledge he knows what is best for us. But, as the parable indicates, we must have faith in God's wisdom and justice. As we continuously pray, the Lord will take everything into consideration and work out his response to our concerns and needs in accordance with his will.

Our prayers should be unrestrained and passionate, seeking the Lord from the depth of our being. (Jeremiah 29:13) In Paul's epistles to the churches, he repeatedly encouraged the people to be faithful in prayer, telling them that they should pray continually, on all occasions, with all kinds of prayers and requests. (Romans 12:12; Ephesians 6:18; I Thessalonians 5:16-18) He told the Colossians that their lives should be devoted to prayer. (Colossians 4:2) Paul knew his weaknesses and his need for a viable prayer life, which would serve as a perpetual source for divine grace. As Paul continuously prayed, he realized that God was in his daily activities, as well as the plans for his future.

The lack of persistent prayer is a weakness in the lives of both individuals and the Church. A sporadic and superficial prayer life is an obstacle to spiritual discernment and God's leading. Without abiding prayer we allow our emotions to rule us, and this opens the door to sin. The Church, which is influenced by societal changes, is always confronted with issues to consider; therefore, prayer must be persistent in order to know God's will. The prayers of individuals and the Church tend to be short lived and lacking depth and passion. Occasional prayers that lack intensity and emotion are void of assurance and power. This weakness also decreases faith and the ability to experience God in our daily activities. To be called by Jesus Christ is to be brought into communion with God, which is a relationship that is built upon and continues through prayer.

The parable of the *Persistent Widow* speaks about receiving justice in this life, but a more predominant theme is that of earnest and persistent prayer. Those who maintain their communion with the Lord are assured of receiving the grace needed to face challenges and to endure trials. It is inconceivable to believe that we can experience God's gifts apart from a prayer life that speaks to all of our needs. We will never know the mysteries of the Lord, but we can know the power of his presence through our communion with him. And yes, God will ultimately bring justice to his people who cry out to him day and night. The Lord will not turn a deaf ear to the persistent pleas of his children, for it is their tenacious hearts that ignite his compassion and mercy.

Praise and Thanksgiving

The Bible contains numerous expressions of praise and thanksgiving offered up to the Lord. Many of the psalms written by David and other writers reflect thankful and trusting hearts. More recently, are the great hymns and doxologies of the Church that have been sung by Christians over the centuries. These worshipful songs include words, such as:

Praise God from whom all blessings flow; Praise him, all creatures here below; Praise him above, ye heavenly hosts; Praise Father, Son, and Holy Ghost. (Louis Bourgeois, cir. 1510-61; Genevan)

Now we thank all our God with heart and hands and voices, who from our mother's arms, hath blessed us on our way with countless gifts of love, and still is ours today. (Johann Cruger, 1598-62, verse 1)

For the beauty of the earth, for the beauty of the skies, for the love which from our birth, Over and around us lies, Christ, our God, to thee we raise this sacrifice of praise. For the beauty of each hour of the day and night, hill and vale, and tree and flower, sun and moon and stars of light, Christ, our God, to thee we raise this our sacrifice and praise. (Henry Smart, 1813-79, verses 1,2)

Give to our God immortal praise, mercy and truth are all his ways, wonders of grace to God belong, repeat his mercies in your song. Give to the Lord of lords renown, the King of kings with glory crown, his mercies ever shall endure, when lords and kings are known no more. (John Hatton, 1793, verses 1,2)

These verses of praise and thanksgiving are but a few penned by our forefathers in their effort to give God the glory that belongs to him. Such praise has always been an integral part of corporate worship. But how often do we give God praise apart from a structured worship service? Sometimes we forget that every gift, both temporal and spiritual, comes from the Lord. The apostle James reminded the Christian Jews of this when he wrote, "Don't be deceived dear brothers. Every good and perfect gift is from above, coming down from the Father of heavenly lights, who does not change like shifting shadows." (James 1:16,17) The gifts given by God include the opportunities that enable us to improve our lives. If the Lord were to remove his presence from us we would be in despair. This is a truth that we seldom think about, with the result being the lack of thanksgiving and praise. Even the faith that has transformed our life is a gift from heaven. From the moment of our birth we are dependent upon the mercy of God.

In celebration of the Ark of the Covenant coming to Jerusalem, David gave Asaph and his associates a psalm of thanksgiving, which begins with these words: "Give thanks to the Lord, call on his name; make known among the nations what he has done. Sing to him, sing praise to him; tell of his wonderful acts." (I Chronicles 16:8,9) Many of the psalms begin with words of praise and thanksgiving, such as:

> Give thanks to the Lord, for he is good; his love endures forever. (Psalm 107:1)

> Give thanks to the Lord, call on his name; make known among the nations what he has done. (Psalm 105:1)

> We give thanks to you, O God, we give thanks for your Name is near; men tell of your wonderful deeds. (Psalm 75:1)

The apostle Paul always offered up praise and thanks to God. It was the Lord who saved him from his ignorance and the sinful path that he was pursuing, and Paul never forgot God's forgiving and saving grace. It was his practice to enlighten fellow believers of God's abundant mercy, encouraging them to offer up praise. (I Thessalonians 5:16-18; Philippians 4:6) Paul often thanked the Lord for his fellow Christians, whose faith and commitment was a witness to him and others. (Ephesians 1:16; II Thessalonians 1:2) In his instructions to his co-worker Timothy, he said, "I urge, then first of all, that requests, prayers, intercession and thanksgiving be made for everyone." In this charge to Timothy, Paul also emphasized the need to give thanks for individuals in authority positions. (I Timothy 2:1-4)

Whether it is the air we breathe, the beauty of nature, medical technology, or the countless other gifts bestowed upon us by our Creator, everyone should be living with praise on their lips. When we ponder God's miraculous power and infinite love, it is difficult to comprehend why so many people fail to respond with thankful hearts. We tend to lose perspective, believing that gifts result from human effort. This, of course, diminishes the need for God in our lives, which directly impacts upon how we live. When these realities take place we walk a self-serving path that is an obstacle to divine grace.

While teaching an adult Bible class on prayer, I asked the members to share the gifts for which they frequently give thanks to the Lord. To my astonishment, most of the group was struggling with the question. Some of them admitted that they never gave much thought to the many ways in which God is working in their lives. On that particular day I learned how important it is for the Church to weave this topic into its ministry. This class was continued for another week, so that an assignment could be given. Everyone was asked to contemplate the presence of God, both in the world and in their lives. While doing this, they were to make a list of God's gifts and begin offering prayers of praise and thanksgiving. It was suggested that they do this for the entire week between classes to see if their list expanded. When we met again we were all blessed with the gifts that were shared. In fact, there was excitement in the class, for which we offered up praise to the Lord.

Over a two-week period the class learned the importance of taking time to reflect upon the many ways that God provides for us on a daily basis. The realization of God's endless gifts increases our faith and brings us to new spiritual heights. We become more sensitive to the movement of the Holy Spirit and how the gifts of the Spirit sustain, empower and guide us. When we experience the Lord in our daily routines, we are compelled to praise him. Giving God praise and thanks is essential for our spiritual journey, which includes making others aware of his awesome presence and gifts of mercy.

Communal Prayer

Beginning in the wilderness, the Jews were led by God to gather together. Abraham and Jacob built altars in the desert, and it was in the wilderness where Moses established a tent for those making inquiries of the Lord. (Genesis 12:5-8; 35:1-3; Exodus 33:7-11) At a later time, God gave Moses detailed instructions for the building of a tabernacle. (Exodus 35) These gathering places foreshadowed the local synagogues and the temple in Jerusalem. The Jews believed that God called them together for communal forms of worship and prayer. During the ministry of Jesus, people frequented the temple courts for prayer and on mandated holidays. The parable of the *Pharisee and the Tax Collector* reveals that people frequently came to the temple for prayer. (Luke 18:10) After the ascension of Christ we learn that the apostles also met at the temple for prayer. (Luke 24:50-53; Acts 2:46,47; 3:1)

The Spirit of Jesus is present, even when just a few people gather in his name. (Matthew 18:19,20) After our Savior's ascension, his followers came together as a community of believers for the purpose of prayer, mutual encouragement, and support. These meetings prompted questions about leadership and mission that were addressed through prayer. The lives of Jesus' disciples had drastically changed, for they were confused and lacked direction. It was through communal prayer that they sought guidance for their new faith and life. A common practice was meeting together in private residences. This gave them protection from threats, as well as the privacy they needed to pray and discuss the future. Immediately after our Lord's ascension the apostles returned to Jerusalem, to the upper room of a home where they temporarily stayed. This was the first location where they met as a group. (Acts 1:12-14) Both Peter and Paul mention gatherings that took place in other residences. (I Corinthians 16:19; Galatians 4:15; Philemon 2)

The practice of Christians meeting for prayer and mutual encouragement continued, giving the early Church the direction and power that was needed to proclaim the gospel in what was often a hostile environment. It was these fellowships of prayer that kept them steadfast in their faith. Early writings actually reveal Christians searching for opportunities to gather together for the purpose of prayer, worship, and to share their blessings. This is not to suggest that they were in agreement on all matters of doctrine and mission. But they were in one accord concerning their faith in Jesus and the need for communal prayer.

The meetings that were crucial to the early Church are no less important today. However, although congregations meet for worship and social functions, prayer is seldom emphasized or practiced in group settings. Apart from the prayers written in the worship program, few churches set aside time for other forms of congregational prayer. Rather than Christians coming together for prayers of praise, intercession, and guidance, churches find themselves stumbling through important decisions. It is communal prayer that unites people, even when individual desires and opinions differ. Praying together also has a healing effect, especially when conflict exists.

Churches that pray together about their concerns and mission seem to have fewer relational tensions, and this lessens the obstacles that prevent successful ministry. As disciples of Christ we are one body and share one Spirit, a truth which reinforces the need for communal prayer. In a world of secular influences and questionable doctrines, it is crucial that churches engage in corporate prayer. When we become one in prayer we are joined together by the risen Christ, whose Spirit speaks to us both individually and as a fellowship of believers. Church leaders must rekindle the fires that bring people together for the divine wisdom that comes through prayer.

Praying in Jesus' Name

Jesus told his disciples that no one comes to the Father except through him, and he promised that through him their prayers would be answered. He said, "You may ask for anything in my name, and I will do it. Ask and you will receive, and your joy will be complete." (John 14:6,13,14; 16:23,24) Paul wrote that it is through Jesus that we have access to the Father. (Ephesians 2:18) But why must we pray in Jesus' name? How should we understand our Savior's command and the teachings of the apostles?

God sent his Son into the world to share in our humanity and to pay the penalty for our sins. His ministry and mission was a path of suffering that led to crucifixion, and we are forgiven and reconciled to the Father because of what Jesus has done for us. God accepts us because we love his Son and have placed our trust in his atoning sacrifice and promises. Apart from Jesus, we have no merit to stand before the Father. Rather than our good works, it is the redemptive work of Jesus that justifies us before God. As a people redeemed by Christ, we approach the Father through his advocacy. Our prayers are received because Jesus has taken us unto himself and has become our intercessor. Having received his Son into our hearts and lives, God accepts us as his adopted children.

To pray in the name of Jesus is to claim victory over Satan and the forces of evil. To invoke our Savior's name is to acknowledge that we belong to him in body, mind, and spirit. It is a statement that our saving and sustaining grace flows through the love and power of Christ. The Father has given all power and authority to his Son, which includes the final judgment of humanity. It is through the life, death, and the resurrection of Jesus, that the Father is glorified.

An important insight speaking to the intercessory nature of Jesus is the reference to himself as the *Son of Man*. It is not coincidental that he assumed this title during his earthly life, employing it continuously when speaking about himself. The Jews were quite familiar with these words, for the prophet Daniel used them in describing someone in human form appearing on the clouds of heaven. This is Daniel's vision:

> In my vision at night I looked, and there before me was one like a *son of man*, coming with the clouds of heaven. He approached the Ancient of Days and was

led to his presence. He was given authority, glory and sovereign power; all peoples, nations and men of every language worshipped him. His dominion is an everlasting dominion that will not pass away, and his kingdom is one that will never be destroyed. (Daniel 7:13,14)

These words, which were written to Jewish captives in Babylon (605-536 B.C.), have both Messianic and apocalyptic significance. What Daniel saw was a cosmic event in which this *son of man* figure was given authority over all creation. It was a message of hope for the Jews, for they were anxiously awaiting some manner of Messiah from God. To the captives, this was an announcement of future deliverance from foreign bondage. Little did they know the spiritual significance that this prophetic vision held for all creation.

The Book of Enoch communicates images analogous to that of Daniel, with an emphasis upon a universal judgment. (Enoch 46:1-6; 48:2-10; 62:5-16; 63:11; 69:26-29; 70:1) By assuming the *Son of Man* title, Jesus was claiming to be the fulfillment of Daniel's prophecy. It was a statement that he was the figure seen in the vision, that of God's Messiah coming to earth as both Savior and judge over all creation. Toward the end of his ministry, Jesus warned his disciples about the events that would occur at the end of the age. He said, "At that time the sign of the *Son of Man* will appear in the sky, and all the nations of the earth will mourn. They will see the *Son of Man* coming on the clouds of the sky, with power and great glory." (Matthew 24:27-35) Jesus continued by saying that his return will be sudden and when least expected, like a flash of lightning across the sky. These words seem to relate to the vision that Daniel saw.

The mission that began with Jesus' incarnation, being born

into the human family, will reach its fulfillment when he returns to judge the world and usher in God's eternal kingdom. As the *Son of Man*, Jesus completely identifies with the human condition. He has experienced our temptations and suffering, which makes him an understanding and compassionate intercessor before the Father. According to the writer of Hebrews, in Christ we have a high priest who can sympathize with our weaknesses and one who was tempted in every way. (Hebrews 4:15) When Jesus called himself the *Son of Man*, he was expressing a bond with us that is eternal. His human suffering and wounds are forever a part of the Godhead. To those who questioned his authority, Jesus said, "For as the Father has life in himself, so he has granted the Son to have life in himself. And he has given him authority to judge because he is the *Son of Man*." (John 5:26,27) As the *Son of Man*, he has become one with humanity, assuming the position of both mediator and advocate before the Father, who receives us in Jesus' name.

Chapter Three
Content of Prayer

Gift of Love and the Spirit

What we pray for mirrors our understanding of the Scriptures and the Christian life. If the focus of our prayers is upon worldly things rather than spiritual gifts, our lives will reflect this. In addressing this subject with his disciples, Jesus said:

> Which of you fathers, if your son asks for a fish, will give him a snake instead? Or if he asks for an egg, will give him a scorpion? If you then, though you are evil, know how to give good gifts to your children, how much more will your Father in heaven give the Holy Spirit to those who ask him. (Luke 11:11-13)

Jesus assured his disciples that God knew their needs, even before they came to him in prayer. He said that their needs would be met if the kingdom of God was their priority. (Matthew 6:8,33) Rather than secular gifts that are temporary and may even prove to be harmful, Jesus wanted his disciples to have spiritual gifts. He told his followers not to worry about the typical things that concern people. Although such things have their importance, they cannot compare to God's transforming and eternal gifts. Like King Solomon, who asked God for wisdom to rule the people, our petitions should reflect a higher purpose. When we pray for the gifts of God we will receive the Spirit's leading in all areas of life. This was Paul's experience, and he challenged other Christians to pray toward this end, saying:

> Live by the Spirit, and you will not gratify the desires of the sinful nature. For the sinful nature desires what is contrary to the Spirit, and the Spirit what is contrary to the sinful nature. They are in conflict with each other, so that you do not do what you want. But if you are led by the Spirit, you are not under the law. (Galatians 5:16-18)

To live in the Spirit is to be released from both the bondage of sin and the oppressive religious laws created by others. Life in the Spirit enables us to rejoice in our uniqueness and to find peace and joy in God's love and promises. In an effort to guide the Galatians toward such a life, Paul contrasted the sinful nature with the conversion that takes place through the Holy Spirit. Rather than living a self-centered life or one grounded in legalism, Paul urged his readers to pray for the nature of God, which is found in the heart and mind of Jesus. In his letter to the Corinthian congregation, he echoed the teachings and command of Christ, which places love as the most important gift. It was for love that Jesus came to earth, and it is this same love that we are to passionately pursue through prayer. Love is the divine gift that creates a Spirit-filled life and makes all other gifts possible. Paul shared these insights with the church in Corinth:

> If I speak in the tongues of men and of angels, but have not love, I am only a resounding gong or a clanging symbol. If I have the gift of prophecy and can fathom all mysteries and all knowledge, and if I have a faith that can move mountains, but have not love, I am nothing. If I give all I possess to the poor and surrender my body to the flames, but have not love, I gain nothing. Love never fails. But where there are prophecies, they will cease; where there are tongues, they will be stilled; where there is knowledge, it will pass away. And now these three things remain: faith, hope and love. But the greatest of these is love. (I Corinthians 13:1-3, 8,13)

It is one thing to say that we love others, but to truly love all people with a pure heart can be difficult. In the prison system I learned that loving individuals who have committed heinous crimes is not easy, particularly when there is no evidence of remorse. Prisoners have an uncanny way of analyzing staff, and they know when someone is insincere. This is an obvious concern when assuming the role of their pastor. I frequently had to confront negative feelings that resulted from stressful interactions with prisoners. To combat these destructive emotions I persistently prayed for the compassionate and forgiving heart of Jesus. There were times when I fell short in communicating God's love, but prayer always renewed my inner spirit, enabling me to provide the love that touched their lives and gave them hope.

Jesus repeatedly reminded his disciples about the need to love others. He said:

> As the Father has loved me, so have I loved you. Now remain in my love. If you obey my commands, you will remain in my love, just as I have obeyed my Father's commands and remain in his love. I have told you this so that my joy may be in you and that your joy may be complete. My command is this: Love each other as I have loved you. Greater love has no one than this, that one lay down his life for his friends. (John 15:9-13)

Praying for Enemies

It would be interesting to know how many Christians pray for those perceived to be enemies. This question has both personal and international implications. First, are we praying for individuals who seek to hurt us in some way? Also, do we pray for the leaders and people of other countries that our politicians have declared to be enemies? I doubt that many Christians pray for people of other cultures and religions, especially if they are looked upon in a negative way. Actually, one can reasonably assume that there is a universal reluctance to pray for any country that causes us distress or harm. But the failure to pray for our enemies contradicts our Savior's teachings on love. Jesus tells us to love our enemies and to be merciful toward those who offend us. (Luke 6:27-36)

The most difficult lessons to internalize and live are those relating to our enemies. Even in the Church we find Jesus' uncompromising words falling upon deaf ears. We tend to filter the Scriptures according to our desires and agendas, and the command to love all people goes against what is reasonable. Some church members believe that such a love is impossible. When it comes to loving and praying for our enemies, we often set conditions. The rationalization is that we did nothing wrong, and it is the other person or country that must take the initiative toward reconciliation. This response, however, misses the reason for our Lord's command. God has called us to the ministry of reconciliation, and it is we who are to manifest the Lord's inclusiveness and unconditional love. Although few people believe it, the love of Jesus Christ has proven to be a strong weapon against bitterness and hatred. Loving one's enemies will always be a spiritual battle that must be fought on a daily basis.

The parable of the *Good Samaritan* is an excellent example of God's infinite love. Because of racial and religious differences, the Jews and Samaritans had a relationship that was divisive. But in this story, Jesus tells us about a Samaritan who risked his life to save a Jewish traveler who became a victim of violence. The Samaritan did not check the credentials of the victim or ponder the differences between them. All he saw was a person in pain and in dire need of assistance. In fact, the Samaritan did everything possible to comfort the man, even taking him to an inn and paying for additional care. (Luke 10:25-37) According to Jesus, this is the love that we are called to possess and share with others. Our Christianity is put to the test when confronted with our adversaries. These are the times when we discover who we really are and what needs to be changed in our life. The question is, do we even have the desire for a love that sets no boundaries? If so, do we continuously pray that God will give us forgiving and loving hearts?

As previously mentioned, the apostle Peter once asked Jesus a question about forgiving other people. He asked our Lord if he should forgive a person up to seven times. When Jesus informed Peter that he was to forgive seventy-seven times, he was emphasizing that forgiveness has no limits. Peter thought that forgiving someone seven times was more than generous, especially since the teachers of his day set a limit on the number of times that a person should be forgiven. The answer Jesus gave Peter shook the foundations of his understanding of God and Judaism. It is doubtful, however, that Peter's question was asked in the context of Israel's enemies, for that would have been another issue. If there is difficulty forgiving a person not considered an enemy, one can imagine the struggle people have pardoning a true adversary.

The command to love and pray for our enemies is exemplified in the life and teachings of Christ. His death for all sinners was the highest expression of love for one's enemies. This sacrifice was the foundation for his eternal kingdom, which continues to grow through acts of mercy. Earthly kingdoms built upon hatred and war have come and gone, but the kingdom of God's love cannot be destroyed. Can you envision a world in which individuals and countries made reconciliation a priority? Regardless of the circumstances, it is difficult to hate those who reach out to you with concrete forms of love.

Jesus teaches that personal forgiveness rests upon our forgiveness of others. This was emphasized with our examination of the Lord's Prayer in Chapter One. In other passages Jesus said, "If you forgive men when they sin against you, your heavenly Father will also forgive you. But if you do not forgive men their sins, your Father will not forgive your sins." Again Jesus said, "When you stand praying, if you hold anything against anyone, forgive them, so that your Father in heaven may forgive your sins." (Matthew 6:14,15; Mark 11:25) The words given to us by Jesus are clear and uncompromising. Many people fail to understand that forgiveness is a salvation issue, for without God's forgiveness we cannot enter his kingdom.

In his epistles to the churches, Paul repeatedly addressed the subject of forgiveness. To the congregation in Ephesus he wrote, "Be kind and compassionate to one another, forgiving each other, just as in Christ, God forgave you." (Ephesians 4:32; cp. Romans 12:14; I Corinthians 4:12; Colossians 3:13; Philemon 10) The other apostles also stressed the need for forgiveness. Peter told fellow Christians that they should practice humility and compassion and should never repay evil with evil. (I Peter 3:9-12)

The indwelling presence of the Holy Spirit moves us to pray for all people. In other words, when the love of Christ is in us, the desire to forgive is a natural response. It may not be the first emotion, but as we pray, allowing the Spirit to speak to our heart, the anger begins to diminish. When this occurs our desire to pray increases, which in turn ignites the love that is necessary to forgive others. We must remember that forgiveness is supernatural and is only realized through prayer. Whenever we think about casting others aside, we should ponder the love that took Jesus to Calvary. We are all sinners in need of ongoing forgiveness and grace, apart from which no one would be saved.

We must never diminish our past sins or our continuing need for God's forgiveness. Paul told fellow believers that he had been the worst of sinners, even persecuting the first Christians. He said to his friend Timothy, "Christ Jesus came into the world to save sinners—of whom I am the worst. But for that very reason I was shown mercy, so that in me, the worst of sinners, Christ Jesus might display his unlimited patience as an example for those who would believe on him and receive eternal life." (I Timothy 1:15,16) This personal sharing with Timothy says it all, for it reveals that God's forgiving love can change the hardest heart. Like Paul, sinners can leave their past behind them and dedicate their lives to the Lord. Paul's life is a powerful witness and message of hope for individuals who are living in sin.

I have counseled many people whose lives were changed through the prayers and forgiving hearts of others. In fact, I am one of those individuals who was drawn to Jesus Christ through the understanding and compassion of Christians. If it were not for their forgiving spirits and encouragement, I would not have entered the ministry. In the prison system I had the opportunity to mentor an inmate, who upon his release, entered a seminary and became ordained. He is presently working with poor inner city families. A few years after his ordination he contacted me, expressing how God's forgiveness and the prison ministry changed his life. It is through forgiveness that people are offered a new life in Christ, one that can begin with our prayers and expressions of love. When we forgive and pray for other people, the possibilities are endless. Praying for one's enemies is the seed that brings God's reality into the dark world of sin. It is the spiritual force that changes lives and relationships.

Patience

Patience is needed in every area of life, but few people pray for this important attribute. Even when we pray for divine leading, we often lack the patience to wait upon the Lord. We are inclined to anxiously take control of our lives, believing that God is not responding to our prayers. This leads us away from the Lord's will, causing us to make decisions that may take an undesirable path. Our culture conditions us to be action people who take charge and get things accomplished. The mentality that time is money, filters into our personal and spiritual lives and clouds our perspective. In some instances, those who do not possess this ideology find themselves outside of mainstream society.

Patience is a test of our faith in God and of his promises set forth in the Scriptures. Releasing our control to the Lord and waiting upon his wisdom and timing can prove to be very difficult. Like most people, I struggle with patience, finding it rather painful at times. As a goal oriented individual, I set time tables on objectives and accomplishments. Pastors are often in this mode, primarily because of the many facets of their position and the time restraints to get things done. Some clergy organize their worship preparations far into the future, knowing that unexpected emergencies within their congregations may suddenly take up their time. This approach, although in some ways necessary, leaves little room for the patience that God requires of us. When we disregard the need for patience, our lives lack the insights that the Lord offers us.

King David said, "I wait for you, 0 Lord; you will answer, O Lord my God. I waited patiently for the Lord; he turned to me and heard my cry." (Psalm 38:15; 40:1) These words are a reminder that God's wisdom and knowledge are perfect. When we wait upon his providence, we realize that our welfare is his concern. God's plan is to give us purpose, by creating a life for us that makes a difference in the world. Only in serving the Lord and humanity are we truly fulfilled.

Paul spoke about patience in different ways, instructing Christians that patience in suffering builds character, and that character builds hope. He told believers that they must patiently wait for what they have not yet received. (Romans 8:25) According to Paul, we are to clothe ourselves with patience, thereby imparting sensitivity, love, and tolerance toward all people. He urged the churches to live a life worthy of their calling, exhorting them to be humble and gentle, and to bear with one another in loving patience. (Ephesians 4:1,2; cp. I Corinthians 13:4; I Thessalonians 5:14; I Timothy 3:12; Titus 2:12)

Paul used himself as an example of patience, encouraging others to walk in his footsteps. To his friend and co-worker Timothy, he wrote, "You, however, know all about my teaching, my way of life, my purpose, faith, patience, love, endurance, persecutions and suffering." Paul compared life to a race in which perseverance was needed to cross the finish line. (II Timothy 3:10,11; cp. Romans 12:12; I Corinthians 9:24-27; Galatians 6:9; cp. Hebrews 12:1)

The writer of Hebrews informs us that our inheritance comes through patience, and he accentuates this truth by using Abraham as an example. Abraham patiently waited upon the Lord to bless him with many descendants. Although the Lord made a promise to Abraham, patience was required for it to be fulfilled. (Hebrews 6:12,15; 10:36) In similar words, the apostle James taught that patience brings the maturity that is needed to wait upon the Lord's return. He said, "Be patient, then brothers, until the Lord's coming. See how the farmer waits for the land to yield its valuable crop and how patient he is for the fall and spring rains. You too, be patient and stand firm, because the Lord's coming is near." (James 5:7,8) The apostles expected Jesus to return in their lifetime, but they did not know when it would occur. Jesus promises us that he will return, and the need for patience still exists.

James also speaks about the patience of those who suffer for the Lord, which is a message that is repeated by the apostle John in Revelation. To the seven churches in Asia, John wrote, "If anyone is to go into captivity, into captivity he will go. If anyone is to be killed with the sword, with the sword he will be killed. This calls for patient endurance and faithfulness on the part of the saints." (Revelation 13:10; cp. 1:9; 14:12) Peter adds to this lesson on patience by reminding us that perseverance helps us to be effective in both life and ministry. (II Peter 1:5-8)

We are familiar with the patience of biblical characters, such as Moses, Job, and David, and how their forbearance ultimately brought glory to God. But some people say that these examples are far removed from today's society. The belief is that these individuals shared a special relationship with God that does not exist with common people today. Unfortunately, this narrow understanding often becomes a self-fulfilling prophecy. Patience requires faith in God's Word, and without this faith we cannot experience our spiritual potential. When we lack the capacity of calm endurance, we often act on emotion and impulse. Our Lord's apostles were sometimes found doing this, but they came to realize that perfection is found in God's wisdom and timing.

Patience is not an attribute that is emphasized during our developmental years. Much of our education is focused upon knowledge and facts, rather than character building. Even the Church, which should teach the biblical principles of patience, often fails in this responsibility. How many sermons or lessons have you recently heard that relate to this topic? While we may occasionally talk about patience, it is seldom integrated into our prayer life. But those who pray for this gift find themselves enjoying increased contentment and inner peace. The prophet Micah said, "But as for me, I keep watch for the Lord, I wait in hope for God my Savior; my God will hear me." (Micah 7:7) The implementation of these words should be the prayerful pursuit of every believer.

Prayer for Healing

King David prayed, "O Lord my God, I called to you for help, and you healed me. O Lord, you brought me up from the grave, you spared me from going down into the pit." (Psalm 30:2,3) Who other than God knows the depth of our pain and our need for divine intervention? But, how should we understand personal healing? Is it only physical restoration, or does it involve more? The medical profession has stated that healing involves the whole person, which includes the physical, mental, emotional, and spiritual aspects of life. It is important, therefore, to consider each of these areas when contemplating prayer for the healing of oneself or another person. It is equally important to understand life as being more than the present, meaning that our time here is simply a brief pause and prelude to the eternal. Jesus teaches us that life is more than the physical body and the present age, and this is where faith comes into the picture. Physical healing, which we normally focus upon, is only one part of the healing process. Although our bodies are essential in this life, the mortal will not enter God's heavenly realm. King Solomon wrote, "The dust returns to the ground it came from, and the spirit returns to God who gave it." (Ecclesiastes 12:7)

Paul spoke about the destruction of the earthly body, stating that the imperishable cannot enter God's kingdom. He shared these truths with the church in Corinth:

> Listen, I tell you a mystery: We will not all sleep, but we will all be changed—in a flash, in the twinkling of an eye, at the last trumpet. For the trumpet will sound, the dead in Christ will be raised imperishable, and we will be changed. For the perishable must clothe itself with the imperishable, and the mortal

with immortality. When the perishable has been clothed with the imperishable, and the mortal with immortality, then the saying that is written will come true: "Death has been swallowed up in victory." (I Corinthians 15:51-54)

In another epistle Paul told Christians that we live in an earthly tent that will one day be destroyed. He stressed that our eternal home is not made with human hands. (I Corinthians 5:1) More than the other apostles, it is Paul who confronts the issues concerning life and death, and he calls us to look beyond the physical world to the life that God has eternally prepared for us. This is not to minimize human suffering, or to imply that we should covet pain for a spiritual benefit. But Paul discovered that prayer provides a continuing channel for God's comforting and sustaining grace. When physical healing does not occur, we must rely upon God's ever present mercy and power, knowing that he is in the midst of our pain. Just as the Father was with Jesus during his suffering, he also promises to be with us.

We cannot know the mysteries and will of God, and this certainly addresses questions that relate to healing. Christians are taught to seek God's healing touch, which includes praying for ourselves and others. The Lord is concerned about our pain, and he moves us to be concerned about the struggles of all his children. When we pray for another person's healing, it is a manifestation of God's love in us. However, when we realize that healing will not take place, we then ask God to provide his comfort, strength, and peace to the one who is suffering. Regardless how an illness or disease progresses, we pray for the empowering and comforting presence of Almighty God.

Our prayers for healing are incomplete if we only pray for the physical body, for life is more than what we experience in the present. Paul knew that one day he would leave his earthly body and share in the glory of his Savior. To the Christians in Rome, he said, "The Spirit himself testifies with our spirit that we are God's children. Now if we are children, then we are heirs—heirs of God and co-heirs with Christ, if indeed we share in his suffering in order that we may also share in his glory." (Romans 8:16,17) Paul understood that his present suffering could not be compared with the glory that he would realize in God's eternal kingdom. (Romans 8:18) Although he was concerned about his worldly suffering and needs, particularly the things required to serve God, he was certain that his eternal abode was beyond this world. As we continue to pray for healing, let us consider our life within the reality of the eternal.

Sustaining Grace

It is God's abiding presence that strengthens us through life's trials. And here again, we find Paul's thinking at the center of orthodox theology. When believers in Rome were confronted with hardships, he wrote:

> And we know that in all things God works for the good of those who love him, who have been called according to his purpose. If God is for us, who can be against us? He who did not spare his own Son, but gave him up for us all—how will he not also along with him, graciously give us all things? Who is he that condemns us? Christ Jesus, who died—more than that, who was raised to life, is at the right hand of God and is also interceding for us. Who shall separate us from the love of Christ? Shall trouble or

hardship or persecution or famine or nakedness or sword? No, in all these things we are more than conquerors through him who loved us. (Romans 8:28,31,32,34,35,37)

Praying for sustaining grace is an acknowledgment of our total dependence upon the Lord. It is recognizing that we are in God's hands and completely dependent upon divine power and mercy. Sustaining grace is also realized in Jesus, who promises never to leave or forsake us. Paul expressed this truth in a letter to Christians in Corinth:

We are hard pressed on every side, but not crushed; perplexed, but not in despair; persecuted, but not abandoned; struck down, but not destroyed. We always carry around in our body the death of Jesus, so that the life of Jesus may also be revealed in our body. (II Corinthians 4:8-10)

Just before his ascension, Jesus promised his disciples the Holy Spirit, whom the Father would send in his name. (John 14:25-27) In a letter to the universal Church, the apostle John makes reference of an indwelling power that would enable the followers of Jesus to overcome the trials and evil influences of the world. He said, "You, dear children, are from God and have overcome them, because the one who is in you is greater than the one who is in the world." (I John 4:4) In their victory song over Egyptian bondage, Moses and the Israelites sang of the Lord's strength and his sustaining grace in overcoming their enemy. (Exodus 15) In other instances, Samson knew that only God could give him the courage and power to achieve victory over his aggressors. (Judges 16:28) King David frequently verbalized his realization of God's abiding strength and power, with prayers such as the following:

> Hear my cry, O God; listen to my prayer. From the ends of the earth I call to you, I call as my heart grows faint; lead me to the rock that is higher than I. For you have been my refuge, a strong tower against the foe. I long to dwell in your tent forever, and take refuge in the shelter of your wings. (Psalm 61:1-4; cp. Psalm 28:1; 31:1)

Like David, the apostle Paul learned that regardless how hopeless a situation appears, God will provide for our needs. Paul knew through personal experience that the Lord's power is made perfect in human weakness. He was repeatedly faced with challenges and trials that caused him great pain, and it was only God's mercy that sustained him. Paul testified that when we empty ourselves and allow the Spirit complete reign over us, we will receive the fullness of God's grace. But total submission to God is contrary to our natural desires, and this is where prayer is important.

The author of Chronicles encouraged the people to always seek God's strength, remembering his wonders and miracles of the past. (I Chronicles 16:11,12) By recalling God's delivering and sustaining grace of the past, we are encouraged for both present and future help. In other words, if God provided for us previously, then he will certainly offer present and future hope. We are inclined to recognize the Lord's miraculous power in previous generations, yet we have difficulty seeing how God is working in our lives. We look for obvious signs of the Lord's presence, which causes us to miss the Spirit's quiet participation in our daily activities. But when we actively pray for sustaining grace, we will begin to discern God's presence in all that we do.

Many people live either in the past or the future, with the needs of the present being neglected. In the Lord's Prayer Jesus teaches us to focus upon our present needs. This corresponds with his other biblical lessons that relate to our anxieties about the future. The Lord takes us through life one day at a time; therefore, we should seek God's daily grace and trust him for our future. Jesus told his disciples that each day holds enough challenges, without worrying about tomorrow. (Matthew 6:34)

Deliverance from Temptation

Temptation is a reality that is grounded in the presence of personal evil in the world. Despite our good intentions and spiritual maturity, there will always be evil influences that test our faith and keep us in a state of spiritual warfare. King David's sins of adultery and a planned murder, as well as Paul's initial persecution of Christians, are clear examples of how people fall into sin. While some temptations are obvious, others are subtle and less evident. But regardless of their nature, it is pride, greed, lust, and power that overcome people. Submitting to certain temptations may even be the catalyst that destroys our life.

There are temptations that few people recognize, such as those relating to forgiving and loving others. This is particularly true when it involves someone who has offended us. A continuing temptation is that of spiritual complacency and neglect. I doubt that many people pray about the ways in which they neglect their spiritual life. As our world becomes more complex and materialistic, we devote less time to matters of the soul and our spiritual formation. When societies are entrenched in activities and entertainment, there is little desire or time for spiritual reflection and a nurturing relationship with God. To deny this fact means that we are already entangled in the world's influences. An honest self-examination will enable us to prayerfully make the changes that will lead to our spiritual development and service to others.

When Jesus knew that his earthly life was nearing an end, he voiced concern about the temptations his disciples would face, which interestingly included the possible abuse of their authority and power. He also admonished them, saying, "Watch and pray so that you will not fall into temptation. The spirit is willing, but the body is weak." (Matthew 26:41) This warning also cautions us about the power of temptation and the weakness of the flesh.

In the wilderness, Jesus was continuously attacked by Satan. These intense temptations marked the beginning of a ministry that led him to Calvary. Having lived in the flesh and subjected to all manner of temptation, Jesus is able to identify with the human condition. This union with humanity arouses his compassion, which makes his power available to us. The writer of Hebrews said, "For we do not have a high priest who is unable to sympathize with our weaknesses, but we have one who has been tempted in every way, just as we are—yet without sin. Let us approach the throne of grace with confidence, so that we may receive mercy and find grace to help us in our time of need." (Hebrews 4:15,16)

Paul wanted Christians to know that their temptations were common, which dispelled the beliefs of some people who thought that their faith would somehow release them from evil influences. He said, "no temptation has seized you except what is common to man. And God is faithful; he will not let you be tempted beyond what you can bear. But when you are tempted, he will also provide a way out so that you can stand under it." (I

Corinthians 10:13) This is an important truth to internalize and recall, particularly when we feel weak and vulnerable to sinful forces. During such times we must stand firm upon God's promises and claim the victory that belongs to us. But some people flirt with temptation through their actions and lifestyle, and they fall prey to destructive powers.

The war between good and evil is unyielding and may sometimes seem overwhelming. Paul reminds us that we are not simply contending against flesh and blood, but rather against the rulers, authorities, and evil forces in the heavenly realm. (Ephesians 6:12) He warns us to stand strong against temptation by wearing the full armor of God, which includes faith and perpetual prayer. We are told to be cognizant and vigilant of the many forms of evil that seek our demise.

Whether temptation is related to human pride or our infirmities, strength comes to us through the Word, faith, and prayer. When we are in a spiritual battle our entire being is put to the test, as well as our witness to others. Let us not forget that submitting to sin not only affects our life, but also the lives of others. In the desert Jesus was continuously tested, and his failure would have impacted upon humanity. But our Savior prayed and stood firm upon God's Word, and he tells us to do the same. To fall into temptation is to be controlled by sin, and the longer we walk in unrighteousness the more difficult it is to sense the Spirit's movement. While there is opportunity, we must pray that the deceitfulness of sin would not harden the heart. (Hebrews 3:12,13)

Increased Faith

In Mark's gospel account we read about a father who brought his son to Jesus for healing. Jesus first responded by testing the man's faith. He told him that everything is possible for those who believe. The boy's father said that he did believe, but he wanted Jesus to help him with his unbelief. (Mark 9:23,24) This statement, although it seems to be a contradiction, reflects the struggle that people have with faith. In a way, the man was saying that he wanted to believe, but it was a struggle for him.

Jesus repeatedly addressed faith issues as he interacted with the people. Thomas, who was not with the apostles when Jesus first appeared to them after his resurrection, had difficulty believing that Jesus rose from the dead. He told the apostles that he would only believe if he could place his fingers in the wounds of our Savior's pierced body. After all, seeing is believing, and Thomas wanted to be certain that the impossible occurred. Jesus later came to Thomas and said, "Put your fingers here; see my hands. Reach out your hand and put it into my side. Stop doubting and believe." Jesus then said to Thomas, "Because you have seen me, you have believed; blessed are those who have not seen and yet have believed." (John 20:27,29) In his letter to the church in Rome, Paul stressed the importance of nurturing our faith, stating that salvation is a matter of walking in faith throughout one's lifetime. To his fellow Christians he wrote: "In the gospel a righteousness from God is revealed, a righteousness that is by faith from first to last; just as it is written: The righteous will live by faith." (Romans 1:17)

It is faith that brings spiritual regeneration and a channel through which the Spirit leads us in accordance with God's will. When, in faith, we receive Jesus Christ into our hearts, we become recipients of divine grace and power. This speaks to present experiences, as well as things not yet received. But entrusting our lives to an invisible God can be a spiritual challenge, for it is easier to look to the world for answers. Every day we are confronted with situations that challenge our trust in the Lord. The human suffering caused by disease and wars is enough to raise questions and diminish faith. But we cannot allow the sins of humanity to shatter our life in Christ. We must believe that even in the worst of times God dispenses his grace in ways that we cannot understand. What matters, is that we pray for the increased faith and understanding that will keep us close to the Lord. The world will always let us down, but God is steadfast in his compassion and mercy.

Understanding and Wisdom

An accurate application of the Scriptures is necessary for our spiritual growth and service to the Lord. Understanding the New Testament and how it fulfills the laws in the Hebrew Bible is a primary example. The interpretation of biblical passages has resulted in differences of opinion and divisions within the Church. This is especially true when God's Word does not provide clear answers to the many sensitive and complex issues of our day. The silence of the Scriptures on certain topics opens a wide door for speculation and human emotion. The disunion created by our differences has often had a negative impact on the witness and mission of all faith groups. Conflict even occurs within small Christian circles over such issues as Christian lifestyle.

In his desire to be a just leader of the people, King Solomon asked the Lord for an understanding mind. Realizing the awesome responsibility of leadership, he asked God for wisdom. Knowing that Solomon's heart was pure and that his concern was for others, God granted him the understanding and wisdom that he needed. We must also pray for understanding and wisdom, realizing that our personal development and service to God depends upon our spiritual maturity. When our understanding is aligned with the teachings and mission of Jesus, God's love is revealed in all of our relationships. A discerning mind is one that sees others through the eyes of God, which means that compassion and love take precedence over debated passages of the Bible. Rather than be divided over issues not related to salvation, we should celebrate what unites us, which is the joy and hope that we share in Jesus Christ.

Mark records an interesting conversation involving the apostle John, who came to Jesus upset that others, who were not in their inner circle, were casting out demons in Jesus' name. In his frustration, John said:

> Teacher, we saw a man driving out demons in your name, and we told him to stop, because he was not one of us. "Do not stop him," Jesus said. "No one who does a miracle in my name can in the next moment say anything bad about me, for whoever is not against us is for us. I tell you the truth, anyone who gives a cup of water in my name because you belong to Christ, will certainly not lose his reward." (Mark 9:38-41)

As long as the earthly Church exists there will be different interpretations and understandings, for we have all traveled a different path to where we are on our spiritual journey. It is important, however, that we continue to pray for the wisdom and understanding that allows for objectivity and a heart that mirrors God's love. Pastors quickly realize the different beliefs and traditions that comprise their congregations, and without prayer it would be impossible to bring unity and nurturing in some situations. The prison system is a good example of this reality, for there are individuals from all walks of life blending into one congregation. The goal in every situation is to bring people to an understanding that enables them to accept and love one another in the midst of their differences.

It would be interesting to know how many people persistently pray for the biblical understanding and wisdom that brings spiritual maturity and unity in the Church. These are the prayers that build God's earthly kingdom, thereby hastening the Second Advent of Jesus Christ. As the body of Christ and his priesthood of believers, we are sent into the world to proclaim the gospel message through word and deed. But this can only be accomplished when we understand our faith in the midst of diversity. Although we must not waiver on essential doctrine, wisdom is needed for the many concerns and issues that accompany our changing times.

We need to remember that God loves all people, and he pours out his grace on both the righteous and unrighteous. If this were not true, then the sacrifice of Jesus is limited, and our salvation is questionable. We tend to be ethnocentric in our thinking and approach to ministry, lacking the biblical understanding and wisdom that God requires of us. But through earnest prayer we can overcome these barriers to personal growth and outreach. As God's ambassadors, we are called to minister to people of all cultures and traditions. These challenges are compounded in a world that is constantly in flux.

Praying for the Saints

The prophet Nehemiah came to the Lord, saying, "Let your ear be attentive and your eyes open to hear the prayer your servant is praying before you day and night for your servants, the people of Israel." (Nehemiah 1:6) Like Nehemiah's prayers, Samuel also offered up prayerful concerns for what he perceived to be a sinful request on the part of the people. (I Samuel 12:19) Throughout biblical history we find people praying for each other with all kinds of prayers and requests. This is God's will, which makes it an important teaching and crucial to our spiritual life. In the New Testament Jesus provides the example for intercessory prayer. He prayed for his apostles and for everyone who would be saved through their ministry, saying, "My prayer is not for them alone. I pray also for those who will believe in me through their message." (John 17:20,21) Jesus prayed for the hearts and minds of everyone who would follow in his footsteps. He knew the sinful influences in the world and the need for his disciples to pray for one another.

Paul always encouraged intercessory prayer, and he assured others that they were in his thoughts and prayers. To the Thessalonians he wrote:

> We constantly pray for you, that our God may count you worthy of his calling, and that by his power he may fulfill every good purpose of yours and every act prompted by your faith. We pray this so that the name of our Lord Jesus may be glorified in you, and you in him, according to the grace of our God and the Lord Jesus Christ. (II Thessalonians 1:11,12)

While imprisoned in Rome, Paul asked people of faith to pray for him and all believers. To the Christians in Ephesus, he said, "Be alert and always keep praying for all the saints. Pray also for me, that whenever I open my mouth, words may be given me so that I will fearlessly make known the mysteries of the gospel, for which I am an ambassador in chains." (Ephesians 6:18-20) He also exhorted the Colossians to pray for him and his co-workers, that the Lord would open a door for the gospel. (Colossians 4:2-4) Whether he was asking people to pray for his power to proclaim the gospel or to be delivered from evil, intercessory prayer was at the center of Paul's spiritual life. As disciples and co-workers for the Lord, he believed that we have the responsibility to pray for one another. Every Christian has priestly functions, meaning that we are to encourage and uplift the body of Christ. Paul called upon believers to love all people, but he underscored the need for a Church that is unified through intercessory prayer.

Prayer for the Needy

In a synagogue in Nazareth Jesus stood up in front of the people and read from the Book of Isaiah, saying:

> The Spirit of the Lord is on me, because he has anointed me to preach good news to the poor. He has sent me to proclaim freedom for the prisoners and recovery of sight for the blind, to release the oppressed, to proclaim the year of the Lord's favor. (Luke 4:18,19)

This biblical passage was understood by the Jews to be a prophecy relating to the anticipated Messiah, whom God promised the people. One can imagine the shock and confusion when Jesus claimed to be the fulfillment of Isaiah's words. Although this statement focuses upon spiritual needs, within its meaning is the Lord's concern for the whole person. The birth of Jesus was God uniting with the lost and helpless state of humanity. In response to criticism, Jesus informed the Pharisees that his ministry was that of a physician. He told the religious leaders, "It is not the healthy who need a doctor, but the sick." (Mark 2:17) He wanted them to know that God detested the ritualistic sacrifices that gave the religious elite a sense of pride. Jesus often admonished the Pharisees and scribes for both their condescending attitude toward the poor and their abuse of responsibility and power. He punctuated his call for mercy with a brief lesson, revealing how our compassion and mercy toward others brings us into God's kingdom. He said:

> For I was hungry and you gave me something to eat. I was thirsty and you gave me something to drink. I was a stranger and you invited me in. I needed clothes and you clothed me. I was sick and you looked after me. I was in prison and you came to visit me. I tell you the truth, whatever you did for the least of these brothers of mine, you did for me. (Matthew 25:35,36,40)

Our Savior tells us that whatever we do for the needy, we likewise do it for him. When we reach out to the less fortunate we assume the nature of Jesus Christ, which is love and mercy toward all people. This is what it means to walk in the earthly footsteps of Jesus. Discipleship is a sacrificial life that seeks to glorify God by doing his will, which is pursuing the life of a servant. True disciples are ministers of mercy, who penetrate the world with concrete forms of love. Like the salt of the earth, we are to make a difference, bringing comfort and hope to those who are struggling in life. We are the Lord's healers and purifiers, called to dispense God's love.

God wants transformed hearts that beat for the lost and needy. How can we be followers of Christ if we do not live in a manner that exemplifies his humility and service? Rather than a building, the Church is a movement that is empowered by God's love, reaching out beyond its institutional structures to touch the lives of those in need. We care about others because we possess the heart and mind of Christ. We are not called to be religious, but rather to be involved. God beckons us to be ministers of love and healing. Like our Lord, we are in the business of transforming and restoring broken lives. The Church is a hospital for life's wounded and dying, and Christians are the emergency room workers. Our discipleship requires us to be weak with the weak, vulnerable with the vulnerable, and powerless with the powerless. Only when we place ourselves in another person's position can we begin to understand their struggles. It is our identification with human need that impels us to pray and become involved. Jesus wants us to prayerfully follow his sacrificial path, offering God's healing and reconciliation.

In his book titled *Only Jesus*, Luis M. Martinez provides insights into the compassion of Jesus:

> When the Lord descended from heaven, he received that doleful inheritance of human lineage. He took upon himself our miseries; He burdened himself with the immense weight of our grief...all the sins of the world, all the abominations of the earth with their incalculable number, their infinite malice, their abysmal ingratitude, accumulated in the heart of Christ, oppressing it and overflowing in torrents of bitterness and blood on that night in Gethsemane. Hear, listen: My soul is ready to die with sorrow. Look, contemplate: His sweat fell to the ground like thick drops of blood. (Martinez 1962, 11)

We are to share in the redeeming work of Christ, and this binds us to human suffering. In Jesus Christ love has no limits or geographical boundaries, for everyone is our neighbor. When the compassion of Jesus fills the heart, we become blind to human differences. Our focus is only upon alleviating suffering and bringing hope in the midst of darkness. When we love all people there is an inner peace that assures us that we have assumed the image and mission of Christ. We are sent out to be vessels of mercy to one humanity, thereby walking in the footsteps of Jesus. Just as Jesus gave his life for the world, our compassion and prayers exclude no one.

Christian Unity

Although Christian unity is taught in the Scriptures, it is seldom stressed in church ministries, and the result is the lack of prayer for the oneness that God commands. Rather than focusing upon our unity in Jesus Christ, we sometimes use our differences as weapons to attack one another. Whether in a local congregation or in a broader sense, Christians need to set aside their suspicions and celebrate the forgiving and saving love of Jesus Christ. No spiritual group has penetrated the depths and mysteries of God, and no church possesses all the answers to life's perplexities. The realization of this should bring unity rather than division.

Christian unity has its genesis in a triune God, who emptied himself to unite with humanity. The cost of this unity is found in the sacrifice of Jesus, in which an agonizing death took place within the Godhead. It was for unity that Christ died, and it is for unity that the Church lives. The wounds of our Lord forever communicate the inclusiveness of the gospel message. Regardless of our differences, we are to live in harmony with one another, proclaiming the gospel of one Church and one Savior. Paul told believers in Rome that they were to do what is right in the eyes of everyone and to be willing to associate with individuals of low position. (Romans 12:15-18) He repeatedly emphasized that we share one faith and one baptism, and that we must keep the unity of the Spirit through the bond of peace. (Ephesians 4:3-6) Paul's epistles state that Christian unity is God's command for everyone who professes Jesus Christ as Lord and Savior.

The gathering of Christians is to be a fellowship of sensitivity, understanding, tolerance, and compassion. The uniqueness of each person is divinely given and precious to the Lord. In fact, it is our differences that enable us to experience God's creative power in the world. For Paul, harmonious fellowship is an absolute if we are to walk in truth and profess discipleship. There are many folds within the body of Christ, but there is one Shepherd of the sheep. (John 10:16) Therefore, we must be a sanctified people, who are united in the love and mission of Jesus Christ. This means looking beyond our differences to a higher purpose, which is the salvation of souls. (Philippians 2:1-4)

Jesus taught his disciples that we do not love God if we fail to love one another, for the two are inseparable. To see division in the Church for any reason is a tragedy that must be confronted through prayer. One can understand why many people view the Church as hypocritical, believing that it does not practice what it preaches. When we fail to unite in the essentials of our faith, we diminish our witness in the world. Every Christian should pray for the spirit of ecumenism, which begins within their spiritual circle.

Conclusion

A sporadic and shallow prayer life stifles our spiritual growth and ability to serve the Lord. While a lack of faith may be an issue, secularism and the distractions in life are also factors. In a society that is increasingly becoming materialistic and activity oriented, communion with God is not a priority. This is sometimes true with clergy, whose lives are a reflection of the world we live in. Simply stated, we choose our priorities and the time given to activities, and prayer is not at the top of the list. Like the parable of the *Four Soils*, God's Word often falls into an infested jungle, where competing interests kill any chance for spiritual development. We get caught up in so many things, that we do not have time to feed our soul.

Struggles relating to prayer begin at an early age, for children are seldom taught the importance of prayer, and this lack of understanding and nurturing carries into adulthood. In addition to an emphasis upon worldly pleasures, society teaches that we should be action people and achievers. Regardless where we are on the educational and socioeconomic ladder, this mentality has taken root. While this thinking may bring credence to the importance of a work ethic, it does not address one's spiritual needs.

Some people believe that God is not concerned about our lives, and these feelings are often reinforced during times of trial and personal loss. After all, if the Lord loves us, why do such tragedies occur to people of faith? But the Scriptures do not teach that Christians are delivered from adversity. The martyrdom of the apostles and the persecution of countless Christians over the centuries tell us a different story. Our ultimate example is Jesus, who endured incomprehensible suffering during his brief earthly life. We also know the tragedies that beset today's Christians in their daily lives. We were never promised a life without trials, but we have a God who, in his compassion, experiences our pain and promises his sustaining grace and ultimate victory.

The lack of faith is another cause for one's inadequate prayer life. As we previously noted, some individuals equate the level of personal faith with how the Lord should respond to their needs. If God does not answer according to their desires and expectations, they conclude that faith has no purpose and that prayer is fruitless. Such people set the agenda and dictate how God should meet their needs. Rather than trusting in God's wisdom, they alienate themselves from the grace that God offers.

We are also inclined to seek solutions to our problems within the temporal realm. While the Lord has gifted us with worldly channels for divine wisdom and grace, we must realize that this world is imperfect and limited in terms of providing answers and meeting our needs. When our trust in God is replaced with human reasoning and secularism, prayer is seldom employed. This, of course, marks the beginning of a long destructive path in which we obstruct the movement of the Holy Spirit. The Jewish prophets stated that anyone who does not call upon the Lord will reap the results of their neglect. (Zephaniah 1:4-7) Concerning the leaders of nations, Jeremiah wrote, "For the shepherds are senseless and do not inquire of the Lord; so they do not prosper, and all their flock is scattered." (Jeremiah 10:21) Christian leaders are given the responsibility to convey the importance of prayer to their congregations, which includes teaching them how they should approach the Lord, as well as the spiritual gifts that God desires them to possess. Just as Jesus taught his disciples how to pray, the Church must follow in his example.

Jesus told his disciples that they would face many trials, but he assured them of grace and victory. He said, "In the world you have tribulation, but be of good cheer, for I have overcome the world. He who is in you is greater than he who is in the world." (John 16:33; I John 4:4) It is through communion with God that we are given the inner peace and strength to endure life's difficulties. This is why Peter tells us to cast all of our anxieties on the Lord. (I Peter 5:7)

Rather than trying to be great communicators, we should approach God as the dependent children that we are. Instead of lengthy and eloquent prayers, the Lord desires an honest and pure heart. My personality is rather straight forward, and I usually share my thoughts and feelings with others. This may not always be the best approach when conversing with people, but I find it cleansing in my prayer life. I rejoice that Jesus tells us to refrain from empty repetition. (Matthew 6:6,7) While we must not judge the prayers of other people, it is comforting to know that the Lord welcomes succinct and simplistic prayers. What matters is our righteousness and the purity of our heart. The psalmnist wrote, "The eyes of the Lord are toward the righteous, and his ears toward their cry." (Psalm 34:15) The Lord will not turn his back on the righteous, who call out to him in humility. This certainty of God's presence should fill us with peace and joy. To the church in Philippi, Paul wrote, "Do not be anxious about anything, but in everything, by prayer and petition, with thanksgiving, present your requests to God. And the peace of God, which transcends all understanding, will guard your hearts and your minds in Christ Jesus." (Philippians 4:6,7) The more we commune with the Lord, the more we realize his power and love.

Appendix

Topical Index on Prayer

The following scripture passages do not reflect an exhaustive resource on prayer; however, they do provide insights that offer excellent tools for personal development and teaching.

God Listens to Our Prayers

Exodus 6:5; 22:23; 33:17; Deuteronomy 4:7,29; I Chronicles 28:9; Isaiah 30:19; 58:9; 65:24; Jeremiah 29:12,13; 33:3; Psalm 3:4; 6:8,9; 9:10; 10:17; 18:6; 21:2; 28:6; 31:22; 55:17; 66:19; 102:17; 116:1,2; 118:5; 119:26; 145:18; Zechariah 13:9; James 4:8; 5:16; I John 5:14,15

Seek God While There Is Opportunity

Psalm 32:6; Isaiah 55:6; Hebrews 4:7

Prayers of the Righteous

Job 8:5,6; Psalm 34:15,17; 145:18-20; Proverbs 10:24; 15:8,9,29; Jeremiah 29:12,13; Matthew 6:5-8; John 9:31; Hebrews 5:7

From the Heart

Psalm 119:58; 130:1,2; Lamentations 3:41

Solitude and Silence

Matthew 6:5,6; 14:23; 26:36; Mark 1:35; 6:46; Luke 5:16; 6:12; 9:28; 22:39-41

Righteous Relationships Are Necessary

Matthew 6:14,15; Mark 11:25; I Peter 3:7

Caution Urged

Ecclesiastes 5:2; Matthew 6:7-9

Intercession of the Holy Spirit

Romans 8:26,27

Pray Continually

I Chronicles 16:11; Psalm 55:17; 86:3; 88:1; Daniel 6:10; Luke 2:37; 18:1; 21:36; Acts 6:4; 10:1,2; Romans 12:12; Ephesians 6:18; Colossians 4:2; I Thessalonians 3:10; 5:17; I Timothy 2:8; 5:5

Pray About Everything

Philippians 4:6; I Peter 5:7

Pray in the Spirit

Ephesians 6:18; Jude 20

For More Workers

Matthew 9:35-38

Fervent Prayer

Psalm 130:1; Jeremiah 29:13; Colossians 4:2

Persistence

Luke 11:5-8; 18:1-7

Patiently Waiting upon the Lord

Psalm 38:15; 40:1; Lamentations 3:25,26; Micah 7:7

Approaching God in Humility

Leviticus 26:40-42; II Chronicles 7:14; Psalm 9:12; 10:17; Luke 18:10-14; James 4:10

Praying in Faith

Psalm 9:10; 22:4-5; 37:5; 38:15; Matthew 21:22; Mark 11:24; Hebrews 4:16; 10:22,23; 11:6; James 1:5-8

In the Name of Jesus

John 14:13,14; 15:16; 16:23-25; Ephesians 2:18

Giving Thanks

Psalm 23:1; 50:14; 75:1; 105:1; 107:1; 117:1,2; Daniel 6:10; Matthew 14:19; 26:26,27; Mark 8:6,7; 14:22,23; Luke 22:19; John 6:11,13; Acts 27:35; I Corinthians 11:24; Philippians 4:6; I Thessalonians 5:16-19

Confessions and Forgiveness

Leviticus 26:40-42; Numbers 5:6,7; Judges 10:10; I Samuel 12:10; I Kings 8:47-50; II Chronicles 7:14; Ezra 9:5,6,15; Nehemiah 1:4-7; 9:2, 33-35; Job 7:20,21; Psalm 32:3-5; 38:4-6; 40:12; 51:1-4; 69:5; 86:5; 106:6,7; 119:176; Proverbs 28:13; Isaiah 6:5; 59:12,13; 65:2,3; Jeremiah 14:7; Lamentations 3:41,42; Daniel 9:5,6; Matthew 3:1,2; Mark 1:14,15; John 1:8,9

Praying for the Gospel

Ephesians 6:18-20; Colossians 4:3,4

Relating to Temptation

Matthew 26:40,41; Luke 22:39,40

Casting out Evil

Mark 9:28,29

Deliverance from Trouble

Psalm 9:15; 18:3; 34:6,17; 50:15; 77:1,2; 81:7; 86:7; 106:44; 107:6; 143:11; Isaiah 56:9; Luke 21:36

Strength and Healing

Judges 16:28; I Chronicles 16:11; Psalm 9:9; 28:1; 30:2; 31:3; 61:1-3; 105:4; 138:3; Luke 21:36; 22:44

Justice Issues

Psalm 10:17; 22:24; 69:33; 74:10,11, 18-23; 79:10-12; 83:1,2,18; 102:17-20; 115:1,2; 143:11,12; Isaiah 19:20; Jeremiah 18:19-23

God's Will

Matthew 26:39; Luke 1:38; Romans 1:10; I John 5:14,15

Divine Leading

Psalm 31:3; Proverbs 3:6; Jeremiah 31:9

Old Testament Intercessions

Exodus 1:9,10; Numbers 14:19; Deuteronomy 9:25,26; I Samuel 12:19; Nehemiah 1:6; Daniel 9:3,16-19; Joel 2:17

New Testament Intercessions

Romans 1:9,10; Ephesians 1:15,16; 6:18,19; Colossians 1:9,10; 4:3,4; I Thessalonians 3:10; II Timothy 1:3; James 5:16; Revelation 5:8; 8:3

Receiving Through Prayer

Psalm 37:4; Isaiah 30:19; Matthew 7:7-11; Luke 11:11-13; John 15:7,8; 16:23-26; Acts 22:16; Ephesians 3:20; Hebrews 4:16; James 5:16; I John 3:22

Gifts Through Prayer

Psalm 55:16; Proverbs 2:3-6; Ezekiel 36:37,38; Joel 2:18,19,32; Amos 5:4-6; Matthew 7:9-11; Luke 11:13; Romans 10:12,13; I Corinthians 12:4-11; James 1:5

Responses to Prayer

Lamentations 3:57,58; Jonah 2:1-6; Zechariah 10:6; Luke 23:42,43; Acts 4:31; II Corinthians 12:8,9; James 5:17,18

Reasoning with God

Exodus 32:11-14, 32-33; Numbers 14:13-23; Judges 6:36-40; I Samuel 1:10,11

Corporate Prayer

Matthew 18:19,20; Acts 1:12-14

Troubles Make Prayer Difficult

Psalm 77:1-4

House of Prayer

Luke 19:45,46; Acts 3:1

Prayer Removes Fear

Psalm 34:4; Lamentations 3:57; I Peter 5:7

Failure to Pray

Jeremiah 10:21; Hosea 7:7; Zephaniah 1:4-6

Resources

Board of Publication, Lutheran Church in America. *Service Book and Hymnal.* Minneapolis: Augsburg Publishing House, 1958-75.

Bonhoeffer, Dietrich. *The Cost of Discipleship.* New York: Macmillan Publishing Company, 1963.

His Holiness John Paul II. *Crossing the Threshold of Hope.* New York: Alfred A. Knopf, Inc., 1994.

Holy Bible—New International Version. Grand Rapids: Zondervan Corporation, 1978.

Martinez, Luis M. *Only Jesus.* United States of America: B. Herder Book Company, 1962.

Nave, Orville J., ed. *Nave's Topical Bible.* Milford: Mott Media, Inc., 1984.

Nouwen, Henri J. M. *The Way of the Heart.* New York: Ballantine Books, 1981.

Tillich, Paul. *The Eternal Now*. New York: Scribner's Sons, 1963.

Unger, Merrill F., *Unger's Bible Dictionary*. Chicago: Moody Press, 1957-87.

Young, Robert. *Young's Analytical Concordance to the Bible*. Grand Rapids: William B. Eerdmans Publishing Company, 1964.

MORE BY DR. HENRY G. COVERT

Ministry to the Incarcerated
Dr. Covert uses his experiences as both police officer and state prison chaplain to examine the environment of the incarcerated—people who are often forgotten by society. He emphasizes particular areas of inmate stress and how they impact upon the inmate's spiritual formation and the role of the Church in offering encouragement, healing and transformation. He calls for staff education, environmental improvement, and a pastoral presence that facilitates rehabilitation and hope, rather than discouragement and punishment. *(185pp. index. Masthof Press, 2022) $12.00*

Journey to the Next World
Death and the afterlife speak to everyone. Dr. Covert examines our life journey from different perspectives, including the biblical understanding of death and resurrection and the events leading to the Second Advent of Jesus. He reminds us of the many obstacles and destructive forces that are encountered as we journey to our heavenly home. The reader is urged to make preparation by nourishing the inner life with the gifts of the Holy Spirit. This book is educational, spiritually motivating, and encouraging.
(125pp. Masthof Press, 2022) $12.00

www.ingramcontent.com/pod-product-compliance
Lightning Source LLC
Chambersburg PA
CBHW070108080526
44586CB00013B/1228